T0646472

JUN 1 0 1998

The Good Housekeeping
ILLUSTRATED
CHILDREN'S COOKBOOK

The Good Housekeeping
ILLUSTRATED
CHILDREN'S COOKBOOK

Marianne Zanzarella
photographs by Tom Eckerle

Morrow Junior Books
New York

Acknowledgments

This cookbook was made possible by a large group of talented people who worked tirelessly on the project, often in addition to their regular jobs. I am grateful to the team at *Good Housekeeping*, who generously contributed their knowledge and expertise throughout this book. They are: Susan Westmoreland, food director; Susan Deborah Goldsmith, associate director, food department; Karen Alyda Kolnsberg, food department assistant; Maya Kaimal MacMillan, photo editor; Mildred Ying, former food director; Mary Fiore, former managing editor.

I would like to thank David Reuther, editor in chief of Morrow Junior Books, for this wonderful opportunity to create a cookbook that children can grow up with. My gratitude to Andrea Curley, my editor, who was a constant cheerleader throughout this project and who worked so diligently to make it a success. A round of applause to Barbara Fitzsimmons, art director, and Josh Weiss, managing editor, for turning my words into a beautifully designed, easy-to-use cookbook. To my beautiful daughter, Francesca, who became an expert egg cracker and very able kitchen assistant during this project. I knew I had a winner whenever she licked her lips and rubbed her belly after a sample. To Michael, for his willingness to taste and taste and taste again and for his help in getting me out of numerous computer scrapes. My love and thanks to my parents, in whose house I grew up appreciating food and the magic worked in the kitchen. The front door was always open and the table always set for everyone to share.

And a big thank-you to Seana Cameron and the children of Bank Street School in New York City: Oliver Baron, Murrayl Berner, Adam Bloch, Sara Brauner, Shani Brignelle, Michael Fusco, Jean Goto, Emma Grunebaum, McKenzie Haynes, Sarah Jacobson, Theodore Kovaleff, Sam Lenzner, Kimberly Max, Aram Mead, Yuta Otake, Lea Schell, Michael Shane, Sasha Siegelbaum, and Lauren Thomas. Their enthusiastic participation in the book, along with their insightful comments, helped me a great deal.

—Marianne Zanzarella

I would like to express my warm gratitude to the food stylists, Mariann Sauvion and Roscoe Betsill, and their assistants, Grady Best and Michael Pederson, for their beautiful work in preparing the recipes and to the prop stylist, Ceci Gallini, for bringing style and personality to these pages. To those who so generously opened their homes to us—Fred and Abbie Wyman, Susan Simon, Todd Weinstein, and Bruce Astrein—my heartfelt appreciation. Cheers to photo assistants Barry Kornbluh and Tony Israel. But most important, special thanks and applause to all the children who made every day fun and inspiring: Arianne Bernardo, Charles DeCrescenzo, Matteo and Kate Eckerle, Gaia Filicori, Ross Friedland, Miles Haas, Tania Haselwander, Katelyn Kelly-Johnson, Kiril Kirilov, Gregory Luger, Giahnna Parker, Kyra and Sheryl Shetsky, Louisa Thompson, and Nicholas, Tory, and Drew Wyman.

—Tom Eckerle

Text copyright © 1997 by William Morrow & Co., Inc.
Photographs copyright © 1997 by Thomas Eckerle

All rights reserved. No part of this book may be reproduced or utilized in any form or by any means, electronic or mechanical, including photocopying, recording, or by any information storage and retrieval system, without permission in writing from the Publisher. Inquiries should be addressed to William Morrow and Company, Inc., 1350 Avenue of the Americas, New York, NY 10019.

Printed in the United States of America.

1 2 3 4 5 6 7 8 9 10

Library of Congress Cataloging-in-Publication Data
The Good Housekeeping illustrated children's cookbook/Marianne Zanzarella.
p. cm.
Includes index.
Summary: General information on kitchen safety and food preparation accompanies recipes for meals from breakfast to dinner, as well as for snacks, drinks, and desserts.
ISBN 0-688-13375-4
1. Cookery—Juvenile literature. [1. Cookery.] I. Zanzarella, Marianne. II. Good Housekeeping (New York, N.Y.) TX652.5.G526 1997 641.5—dc20 96-18800 CIP AC

FOREWORD

When my two sons were growing up, we spent many afternoons in the kitchen together, usually baking. For the boys, it was half science experiment, half chance to eat an unlimited number of chocolate chip cookies. Despite the occasional disaster—like the time one of them accidentally elbowed a cookie sheet off the kitchen counter, losing most of the batch—we had a lot of fun. Still, I often wished there was a book I could give them that would explain everything they needed to know to get the job done safely and easily—so that they didn't need me in the kitchen, watching their every move. I bet they felt the same way! That's why I'm especially pleased to introduce *The Good Housekeeping Illustrated Children's Cookbook*, the first book in the Good Housekeeping food library aimed at children. Drawing on Good Housekeeping's long history as a trusted reference for grown-up cooks, this easy-to-use guide explains culinary essentials in a fun, accessible format to kids eight and older.

All the basics are here: the right way to measure and substitute ingredients, pick the right cookware for a particular dish, test food for doneness, and (parents will be pleased to know) clean up. An extensive section covers food-handling hygiene and the best and safest ways to use all equipment. And, whether you like burgers, pasta, or desserts, you'll find food here to tempt you. Over fifty delicious step-by-step, kid-tested recipes are included—for everything from crowd-pleasers like brownies and chicken fingers to simple family dinners like roast chicken and glazed pork chops. Each recipe lists the utensils and ingredients you'll need, tells how long you can expect the preparation and cooking to take, and gives a difficulty rating, based on ease of preparation and the amount of adult supervision needed. Many recipes are illustrated with color photographs; some include simple variations to suit different tastes.

After you've tried the recipes in the book, I hope you'll be inspired to create dishes of your own. I know your new skills will bring you a great sense of accomplishment. After all, what could be better than being able to make your own pizza? Enjoy!

Ellen Levine
Editor in Chief
Good Housekeeping

CONTENTS

COOKING BASICS

CONTENTS

RECIPES

BREAKFASTS

LUNCHES

DINNERS

Cooking Basics

◆ ◆ ◆ ◆ ◆ ◆ ◆ ◆ ◆ ◆ ◆ ◆ ◆

GETTING STARTED

SAFETY FIRST

HOW TO COOK

GETTING STARTED

Cooking is a lot of fun! But before you start pulling out measuring cups and mixing bowls, take a few minutes to read through this section.

PREPARING TO COOK

Here's how to get yourself ready to cook.

◆ Always read through the entire recipe before you start to cook. It is a good idea to do this with an adult. That way you can discuss any help you may need while preparing or cooking the recipe and can make sure that you understand the directions.

◆ Discuss the "rules of the kitchen" with an adult. For example, are you allowed to use the stove or oven without supervision? Do you handle a knife safely enough to use it by yourself? And be sure to check whether it is a suitable time for you to be cooking. You may not be able to bake cookies if the dinner roast is ready to go in the oven!

◆ Check your refrigerator and cupboards to be sure that you have all the necessary ingredients and equipment on hand. If you are missing any ingredients you must have to complete the recipe, make a grocery list, noting exactly how much of each item you need to purchase. That way you won't buy too much or too little. If you don't have all the equipment mentioned in the recipe's utensils list, an adult may be able to help you make substitutions.

◆ Since it is much easier to cook when you have a clean and uncluttered work space, take the time to clear off an area so you won't feel crowded.

◆ Use a wooden or plastic cutting board for food preparation. A cutting board protects your countertop or work surface from scratches and possible dents, and it protects your knives. Also, hard surfaces, such as glass, ceramic tile, or metal will dull the edges of your knives. A wooden or synthetic cutting board is soft enough to cushion the edge of a knife blade and not dull it.

SUBSTITUTING INGREDIENTS

Food prepared from scratch tastes the best and is the most fun to make. But sometimes you're in a hurry and don't have a lot of time to spend in the kitchen. In those cases you might think about substituting already prepared ingredients for some of the fresh foods mentioned in the ingredients list. Some of the recipes suggest substitutions, and an adult can help you with this also.

Many of the recipe ingredients lists give alternate product suggestions. Some items in the marketplace—such as mayonnaise, yogurt, and various kinds of cheese—can be purchased in *many* forms, ranging from full fat to reduced fat to fat free varieties. Your diet and taste, as well as your family's, will determine which product you buy and use to prepare the recipes in this book.

CLEANING UP

Some recipes keep you busy from start to finish, while others make you wait for something to cook. A good rule to follow whenever possible is "Clean as you go." A recipe that doesn't require your constant attention (some soups, sauces, or roasts, for example) gives you time to start cleaning up before the recipe is complete.

All the dishes and utensils you used should be thoroughly washed and dried. When you have finished cooking, it is important to put all the ingredients and utensils back where you found them. Any appliances that you have used—as well as the countertop or work area—should be wiped down. If you leave the kitchen clean and neat, you will be welcomed back to cook again!

SAFETY FIRST

Safety may seem boring, but it's *very* important. Cuts and burns can be serious! So read this section carefully to learn safe cooking techniques. They will help you avoid accidents in the kitchen.

RECIPE SAFETY SYMBOL

Within each recipe some steps are marked with a safety symbol to alert you that an adult should be present at these points to supervise or help you with your work. The symbol ▲ indicates that in this cooking step you either will be using a sharp object or you will be using the stove or oven or handling a hot object.

DRESSED TO COOK

It's best to wear comfortable old clothes while you cook. That way you'll feel free and won't worry if you accidentally spill or splash something on your clothing. Make sure, though, that your sleeves are not too long or baggy and that your hair is not hanging down in your face. These could catch on fire or get caught in an appliance. And it's always a good idea to wear an apron. It will help protect your clothing when you cook.

KNIVES

One of the most important tools to a cook is a sharp knife, and in order to prepare many of the recipes in this cookbook, you will need to use one. But if it is not used properly, a knife can be very dangerous. Therefore, a knife must always be used with great caution. Here are some rules on how to use a knife properly and safely.

◆ When you are ready to begin cutting, remember to do so on a cutting board. This will protect your work surface as well as keep the blade of the knife from being damaged.

◆ Make sure the sharp edge of the blade is facing straight down toward the food you are cutting. Grip the handle with all four fingers and hold your thumb gently but firmly against the other side of the handle.

Your other hand acts as the guiding hand; it holds the food being cut firmly down on the cutting board and also helps you regulate the size of the pieces you are cutting. The fingers of your guiding hand should be positioned so that the fingertips are curled back slightly and the thumb is held back as they hold down the food.

◆ Always try to have a flat side on the food you are going to cut; round foods are often hard to keep steady while you cut them. To create a flat surface, take a thin slice off the top or bottom of the food, or cut it lengthwise in half. This flat surface can then be set on the cutting board.

◆ When you are using a knife, it is very important to concentrate on the task you are performing. Don't let yourself get distracted while you are cutting, because it is then that accidents happen.

◆ Always hold the knife by the handle—*never by the blade.*

◆ A sharp knife is actually safer to use when handled properly than a dull one, because less pressure is required to cut through the food. A dull knife can slip when too much pressure is applied to it. So before you begin to cook, ask an adult to make sure that the knife you will be using is sharp.

◆ When you have finished using the knife, lay it on its side on the cutting board. Make sure it is not close to the edge of the counter or table, where it could easily fall.

◆ Always keep the knife visible. If you accidentally cover it with a pot holder or dish towel, you might grab the knife blade while picking up the pot holder or towel and injure yourself.

◆ Do not put a dirty knife in a sink full of dishes where it cannot be easily seen. For your safety and that of others, always wash the knife separately, dry it, and put it away or return it to the cutting board to use again.

◆ When walking with a knife, hold it by the handle with the point of the blade facing down.

GRATERS

In order to prepare some of the recipes in this cookbook, you will need to use a grater. Here are some rules on how to use a grater properly and safely.

◆ Always be very cautious as you rub the food along the rough holes of the grater so that you do not scrape your fingers or knuckles.

◆ When one piece of food gets small, it is a good idea to replace it and continue grating or shredding with another piece so that your hand does not get too close to the surface of the grater.

VEGETABLE PEELERS

In order to prepare some of the recipes in this cookbook, you will need to use a vegetable peeler. Here are some rules on how to use a peeler properly and safely.

◆ Be sure to hold the peeler firmly in your hand. You must also hold the food firmly down on the cutting board. See photograph at right.

◆ Always move the peeler *away* from you as you peel the skin from the fruit or vegetable.

HOT OBJECTS

In order to prepare many of the recipes in this cookbook, you will need to handle hot objects. The following utensils will allow you to do so safely and properly.

Pot Holders Protect You

Pot holders and oven mitts are a must while you cook (see photographs on page 161). They protect your hands from anything hot you encounter while cooking in the kitchen. So remember to pick up a pot holder before you pick up any hot pot, pan, lid, or dish.

Pot holders and mitts also protect you from a hot oven, both racks and interior. So always use them when putting a baking pan or cookie sheet into a preheated oven. Use them when sliding out an oven rack and removing a hot pan or cookie sheet from the oven, too.

One last thing to remember: Always make sure that the pot holders you reach for are dry. Wet or damp pot holders will not protect your hands from the heat and might even cause a steam burn.

Trivets Protect Your Work Surface

Throughout this cookbook you will see trivets listed in the utensils lists; other recipes call for cooling racks (see photographs on page 160). Both these utensils have a similar purpose: They allow you to rest a hot pan or casserole safely on a surface without damaging the surface. A trivet or cooling rack will protect the table or counter-top from the heat of the pot or pan. So always use a trivet or a cooling rack and remember to place it where no one will accidentally bump into it.

STOVES

Whether your kitchen is equipped with a gas or an electric stove, it is important to keep the following safety rules in mind while you are cooking or baking.

◆ Always pay close attention to the recipe you are following as well as to the action you are to perform. Otherwise you may have an accident or ruin the recipe.

◆ Regulate the heat of the stovetop or oven according to the recipe's instructions. If you set the heat too low, the food will take longer to cook than the time indicated in the recipe. If you set the heat too high, the food may burn or scorch.

◆ The heat generated from the burners on the stovetop or from the oven can make the stove itself hot. Be very careful not to touch the stove with any part of your body.

◆ When cooking on top of the stove, make sure that the handles of all of the pots and pans you are using are turned toward the center of the stove. This will prevent you or someone else from bumping into the handles and accidentally spilling the hot contents.

◆ Make sure you remove spoons and other utensils you are using from pots and pans while cooking. The handles can get hot.

◆ Some pot handles get hot during stovetop cooking, too. Remember always to hold the handle of a pan or skillet with a pot holder when stirring the food or removing the pan or skillet from the stove.

◆ Remember to use pot holders or oven mitts to put pans in the oven and to take them out.

◆ When you have completed your cooking, turn off the burners and the oven before leaving the stove. This may sound obvious, but you will often be getting ready to serve the cooked food as soon as you take it off the stove or out of the oven, so it's easy to forget that the heat is still on. Leaving the burners or oven turned on is extremely dangerous! So be safe and don't wait until later. Turn off the heat as soon as the cooking is done.

◆ Stir or turn the food when necessary and do so carefully so that hot liquid or hot fat will not splash out of the pot or pan and burn you.

◆ Follow the cooking times given in the recipe so that you do not undercook or overcook the food.

◆ Some recipes require your undivided attention, while others—generally the ones with longer cooking times—allow you to leave the stove and the food unattended for a while. But even when preparing longer-cooking recipes, you occasionally need to stir the food and to check on it to make sure that it is not cooking too quickly or too slowly.

◆ Whenever you take something out of the oven, close the oven door. Otherwise hot air will escape and the oven temperature will go down, lengthening your cooking time.

◆ Some recipes will direct you to cover a pot with a lid or a baking pan with a piece of aluminum foil. When you remove the lid or unwrap the foil, you will be allowing the steam that has accumulated to escape. It's important to cover your hand with a pot holder when removing the lid from a pan and stand away from the pan so that you do not get burned by this steam. When removing foil, start from the corner that is farthest away from you.

HOT LIQUIDS

In order to prepare many of the recipes in this cookbook, you will need to cook with hot liquids. This section tells you how to do so safely.

Boiling Liquids

Boiling liquids are very dangerous and can cause extremely serious burns. Whenever a recipe calls for you to boil a liquid, it is important for you to:

◆ Use the size pot indicated in the utensils list. If you use a pot that is too small, the liquid can boil over the sides.

◆ Keep a close eye on the pot. A liquid that is boiling is evaporating. If you leave the food unattended, it may boil away or burn.

◆ Keep your face and body a safe distance away when checking on whatever is boiling. Boiling liquid creates steam that can burn you if you get too close.

Stirring Hot Liquids

Whenever a recipe calls for you to stir a hot or boiling liquid, it is important for you to:

◆ Hold the handle of the pot with a pot holder in order to stabilize it.

◆ Stir slowly so that the hot liquid does not splash or spill out and burn you.

◆ Keep your face and body a safe distance away from the pot.

Pouring Hot Liquids

When a recipe calls for you to drain food that has been cooked in boiling water, *do not attempt to do this by yourself. Always have an adult pour the boiled food into the colander to drain the water.* Boiling water is very dangerous! If the boiling water spills or splashes while it is being poured, you may get burned. And the steam from the boiling water can also burn you while you are pouring.

After you have finished cooking a hot-liquid recipe, such as soup, chili, or pasta sauce, you must be very careful when serving it. Use a ladle to remove a portion of the hot food from the pot efficiently and safely. Do not try to hold the pot by the handle and pour the hot food into the dishes. You may drop the pot and burn yourself or get splashed with some of the hot food.

PAN-FRYING

Some of the recipes in this cookbook call for you to pan-fry food—to cook it in an uncovered skillet using a small amount of fat. Since the oil used during this type of cooking is hot, it is dangerous. Therefore, it is important that you:

◆ Make sure that the food to be cooked and the utensils to be used are *dry*. If any moisture combines with the hot oil in the pan, it will cause the oil to spatter and bubble up, and the oil can burn you. Therefore, pat pieces of meat, fish, or poultry with a paper towel to absorb any moisture before they are placed in the hot oil.

◆ Always stay a safe distance away from the skillet when adding the food to the hot oil just in case the oil spatters.

◆ Do not leave the stove while heating the oil. If the oil becomes too hot, it begins to break down and can eventually catch fire.

◆ Using a fork or tongs (see photograph on page 154), place the food in the hot oil gently. If you drop the food into the skillet, it may cause the oil to splash up and burn you.

APPLIANCES

While you are preparing some of the recipes in this cookbook, you will be using electrical appliances, such as a blender, food processor, or mixer. When you do, keep the following safety rules in mind.

◆ Keep any electrical appliance *away* from water, including the sink.

◆ Do not touch any electrical appliance with your wet hands or you may get a shock. Always keep a dish towel close by while you prepare the recipes so that you can dry your hands.

◆ Always assemble an electrical appliance first; then plug it into an electrical outlet. That way you cannot accidentally turn on the appliance and hurt yourself if you touch the on button or switch by mistake.

◆ When you are finished with an electrical appliance, always unplug it before you disassemble it. Otherwise you may accidentally turn it on and hurt yourself.

◆ After you have taken the appliance apart, wipe it down with a damp cloth or sponge. *Never* place the motorized part of the electrical appliance in a sink full of water.

Using a Blender

A blender is an electrical appliance with a tall, narrow lidded container that is fitted with short rotating blades in the bottom of the container (see photograph on page 160). Blenders can have up to sixteen speeds and are used for mixing drinks and for making purees and sauces. When using a blender, remember:

◆ Keep the lid on while the blender is in use.

◆ Never fill a blender more than half full with hot liquid. When you turn the blender on, it can overflow and burn you. Leave the center top open to allow steam to escape.

◆ Always wait for the blades to come to a complete stop before removing the lid or inserting a spatula to scrape down the sides of the container.

◆ *Never* put your hand into the blender container while it is operating

Using a Food Processor

A food processor is an electrical appliance consisting of a plastic work bowl with a cover and feed tube that sits on a powerful motor with a protruding shaft (see photograph at right). Standard attachments include a steel blade used for chopping, mixing, blending, and pureeing; a plastic dough blade for breads; a shredding disk; and a slicing disk. When using a food processor, remember:

◆ The steel disks are very sharp and should be handled with great care. The steel blade is equally sharp. When inserting the blade, hold it by the plastic center and place it on the shaft until it fits securely in place.

◆ Depending upon the recipe, ingredients can be either placed in the work bowl or added through the feed tube. If you are placing ingredients in the work bowl, make sure you turn the lid completely to close it. Otherwise the food processor will not start.

◆ When your processing is finished, wait for the blade to come to a complete stop. Unplug the machine and remove first the cover of the work bowl, then the work bowl. Carefully remove the blade, holding it by the plastic center and lifting it out.

Using a Mixer

A mixer is an electric appliance that is used to beat, whip, or mix such foods as cake batter, cookie dough, or cream (see photographs on page 160). Both portable and stationary mixers come with a set of beaters or a flat, open paddle type of beater. The beaters are inserted into the motorized head of the mixer. When using a mixer, remember:

◆ *Never* put your hands into the mixing bowl while the mixer is on.

◆ Even when on low speed, a mixer is fast. Therefore, when adding dry ingredients, do so slowly so that they do not splash out of the bowl.

◆ When you want to scrape down the side of a mixing bowl while preparing a recipe, turn off the mixer and wait for the beaters to come to a complete stop before scraping.

◆ Never start to remove the beaters until you have turned off the mixer and unplugged it.

FOOD HANDLING

You will notice that whenever you handle a raw onion while preparing a recipe, you are instructed to be careful not to put your face too close to it or to wipe your eyes with your hands. This is because onions usually make your eyes tear or sting if you get too close or get onion juice in them. It is a good practice to wash your hands before continuing with the recipe if you handle an onion.

It is essential that you follow these food handling guidelines as well. The following rules will reduce the risks of spreading bacteria while you are preparing the recipes.

◆ Before you begin food preparation, always wash your hands with hot, soapy water; then rinse and dry them thoroughly. Wash them again after handling raw meat, poultry, and fish as well as fruits and vegetables.

◆ Always prepare foods on a clean work surface and always use clean utensils.

◆ If you are preparing a recipe that calls for meat or poultry plus vegetables, thoroughly wash knives, cutting boards, and utensils with hot, soapy water when switching from meat or poultry preparation to vegetable preparation.

◆ Don't put cooked foods on the same plate that held raw meat or poultry. Raw meat or poultry juices should never touch cooked food either in the refrigerator or during food preparation.

◆ Utensils that have touched raw meat or poultry should be washed with hot, soapy water before they are used for cooked food.

◆ Wash all fruits and vegetables with running cold water before you begin your recipe preparation.

◆ Keep all raw, fresh food stored in the refrigerator until you are ready to use it. Your refrigerator should be set at 40° F or colder. Your freezer should be set at 0° F or colder. (You can purchase a refrigerator/freezer thermometer to check these temperatures.)

◆ Throw out any meat, poultry, or fish that looks discolored or smells bad.

◆ Thaw any frozen meat, poultry, or fish overnight in the refrigerator, not at room temperature.

◆ Remember to keep cold foods cold, hot foods hot. Perishable foods should not be kept at room temperature longer than 2 hours. Food that has been left at room temperature longer than 2 hours should be thrown out. If you live in a warm climate, discard food left at room temperature after 1 hour.

◆ If you have prepared hot food for eating later in the day, pour it into a shallow storage container, cover the container loosely, and refrigerate it immediately. If it is a large quantity of food, place it in several shallow food storage containers. When it is time to reheat the food, do so thoroughly, until the food is hot and steaming, or until it reaches a temperature of 165° F.

◆ Refrigerate or freeze any leftovers promptly.

Food must be thoroughly cooked in order to kill harmful bacteria that can cause illness.

Throughout this cookbook, tests for doneness and visual descriptions of cooked foods are given to help you determine if a particular food is cooked fully. While the individual recipes will indicate how to test a specific type of food for doneness, here are some general guidelines to keep in mind.

◆ Ground meats and ground poultry that are made into patties or loaves or are crumbled should be cooked until no pink color remains and the juices run clear.

◆ Chicken and turkey, both whole and parts, should be cooked until no pink color remains and the juices run clear. The color of the flesh will be opaque white, not translucent pink.

◆ Pork, both roasts and chops, should be cooked until no pink color remains and the juices run clear.

The use of thermometers, either meat or instant-read, will help verify that the proper degree of doneness in cooking meats and poultry has been reached. Even though roasting chickens often come with "pop-up" temperature indicators, it is a good idea to test the temperature with a conventional thermometer.

PUTTING OUT A STOVETOP FIRE

Anytime you are using the stove or oven to cook, an adult should be present. A safety symbol ▲ beside a step indicates that an adult should be there at these points to supervise or help you.

◆ If a cooking fire starts, *never* pour water on it.

◆ If a pot or pan of food catches fire, using a pot holder, very carefully slide a lid over the pot or pan and turn off the stove.

◆ If a fire starts in the oven, close the oven door and turn off the oven.

◆ **If the flames do not go out *immediately*, turn off the gas, shut the door, and leave your apartment or house. Then call the fire department from a neighbor's phone.**

HOW TO COOK

HOW TO USE THIS COOKBOOK

You will be seeing some codes as you prepare the recipes in this cookbook. This section explains what each of them means.

Degree of Difficulty Ratings

Each recipe in this cookbook is rated Easy, Moderate, or Difficult. The difficulty rating is based on the types of cooking techniques you will use and the amount of adult supervision you may need to prepare the recipe. The rating system will help you choose a recipe that you will feel comfortable preparing. As you make more of the recipes and gain confidence in your culinary skills, you will want to try the challenging recipes. Even the difficult ones become easier the more times you prepare them!

Preparation Time Clocks

Included in each recipe are clocks that show the approximate amount of time it will take you to do the preparation steps of the recipe as well as the amount of time it will take to do the actual cooking. A total time is given so that you will know how long the recipe takes from beginning to end and can gauge your time properly. The cooling times in the baking recipes have not been included because they vary from food to food.

Servings and Yield Codes

"Servings" tells you how many *servings* you will get from a recipe. For instance, "SERVINGS: 4" means that the recipe will make enough food to feed four people.

"Yield" indicates how large a *quantity* of food a recipe will make. The number of servings you then get will depend on how much of the food each person eats.

If you need to serve more people than the servings code indicates that you can, you may be able to increase the amounts given for the ingredients to make more food. If you are serving fewer people, you may be able to reduce the amounts given for the ingredients to make less food. Ask an adult to double-check you.

Glossaries

In the back of this book there is a glossary that lists the cooking terms and procedures used in the recipes and explains what they mean. If you are not sure about a cooking term that you come across in a recipe, you can look it up there. It is probably a good idea to look up the cooking terms that seem familiar, too. You may be surprised by what you don't know about even the most obvious ones!

In the back of the book there is also a photographic glossary of cooking utensils that you will be using to prepare the recipes in this cookbook. They are labeled so that you can find them easily.

GETTING READY TO COOK

You've read carefully through the "Getting Started" and "Safety First" sections and picked out a recipe to prepare. Now you are ready to start!

1. Gather all the utensils and ingredients listed at the beginning of the recipe.

2. Measure out all the ingredients listed in the ingredients list. If you have enough 1-cup graduated measuring cups, you can leave each dry ingredient in a separate cup after you have measured it out. If you do not have enough measuring cups, pour each dry ingredient as you measure it into a small bowl and then measure out the next ingredient. (Pages 13–14 give you step-by-step instructions on how to measure different types of food.)

3. Arrange the measured ingredients on a tray or baking pan in the order in which they are to be used in the recipe. Then, while you cook, remove each container from the tray after you have used its contents. Not only does this keep you organized, but it prevents you from forgetting to use an ingredient.

HOW TO COOK

This section reviews basic cooking methods that ensure that a recipe will turn out well.

Measuring

Successful recipes depend upon accurate measurements. Here are instructions for measuring various kinds of food.

Dry Ingredients. To measure such dry ingredients as flour, sugar, bread crumbs, and rice and such solid ingredients as shortening or peanut butter, use a set of graduated measuring cups consisting of ¼-cup, ⅓-cup, ½-cup, and 1-cup measures or a set of graduated measuring spoons consisting of ¼-teaspoon, ½-teaspoon, 1-teaspoon, and 1-tablespoon measures (see photographs on page 155).

◆ To measure *flour*, lightly spoon the flour into a graduated measuring cup or measuring spoon. Level off the surplus flour with the straight edge of a knife or spatula. Do *not* pack the flour into the measuring cup.

◆ To measure *sugar*, lightly spoon the sugar into a graduated measuring cup or measuring spoon. Level off the surplus sugar with the straight edge of a knife or spatula.

◆ To measure *brown sugar*, spoon the brown sugar into a graduated measuring cup or measuring spoon, pressing it down with the back of the spoon to pack it. Level off the surplus brown sugar with the straight edge of a knife or spatula. Packed brown sugar will hold its shape when emptied from the cup or spoon.

◆ To measure a *pinch*, squeeze the ingredient between your thumb and forefinger. A pinch is equal to about $\frac{1}{16}$ teaspoon.

◆ To measure a *rounded spoonful*, scoop out the ingredient with the measuring spoon. But don't level off the surplus. The amount of food in the spoon should be slightly higher than the edge of the spoon.

Liquids. To measure such liquids as milk, water, juice, and oil, use liquid measuring cups that come in a 1-cup, 2-cup, 4-cup, and 8-cup capacity and are marked for measuring smaller amounts, or use graduated measuring spoons (see photographs on page 155).

◆ To measure a *cupful* of a liquid, place the liquid measuring cup on a level surface and pour in the liquid to the desired line, reading the measure at eye level.

◆ To measure a *spoonful* of a liquid, slowly pour the liquid just to the top of the measuring spoon without letting it spill over.

Don't measure liquids over the mixing bowl; you may spill extra ingredients into the bowl.

Butter and Margarine. Butter and margarine wrappers are marked off in teaspoons and tablespoons. To measure butter or margarine, just cut off the amount needed with a paring knife, following the guidelines on the wrapper. A $\frac{1}{4}$-pound stick of butter or margarine measures $\frac{1}{2}$ cup, or 8 tablespoons.

Equivalent Measurements

1 tablespoon = 3 teaspoons
$\frac{1}{2}$ tablespoon = $1\frac{1}{2}$ teaspoons
1 cup = 16 tablespoons
$\frac{1}{2}$ cup = 8 tablespoons
$\frac{1}{3}$ cup = 5 tablespoons plus 1 teaspoon
$\frac{1}{4}$ cup = 4 tablespoons
1 gallon = 4 quarts or 8 pints or 16 cups
1 quart = 2 pints or 4 cups
1 pint = 2 cups
1 pound = 16 ounces
$\frac{3}{4}$ pound = 12 ounces
$\frac{1}{2}$ pound = 8 ounces
$\frac{1}{4}$ pound = 4 ounces

Using Eggs

When a recipe calls for you to use an egg, there are a few things you need to know.

Sizes of Eggs. Eggs come in several different sizes. When you buy a carton of eggs at the grocery store, the carton indicates whether the eggs inside are "small," "medium," "large," or "extra large."

The recipes in the dessert section are based on *large* eggs. Eggs of other sizes may be used in those recipes where "large" is not specified.

Temperature of Eggs. It is important when you bake to have the eggs at room temperature. To bring them to room temperature, take the number of eggs you need for the recipe out of the refrigerator and place them in a bowl of warm water for 5 minutes. Dry them off before using.

How to Crack an Egg. It is always a good idea to crack the eggs needed for a recipe into a separate bowl before you add them to the other ingredients. To crack an egg, hold the egg in one hand and then gently but firmly tap the middle of the shell against the rim of a small bowl or cup until the shell cracks. Holding the egg over the bowl, place your thumbs on either side of the crack. Pull the shell apart until the egg falls into the bowl. It doesn't matter if the yolk breaks. If you get a piece of shell in the bowl, use a teaspoon to lift it out.

Washing Leafy Vegetables and Fresh Herbs

When you purchase green leafy vegetables, salad greens, or fresh herbs, they are often sandy and gritty. It is very important to take the time to clean them thoroughly so that they do not ruin your recipe.

To wash them using a *mixing bowl,* place the bowl in the sink. Place the leafy vegetables, salad greens, or fresh herbs in it. Fill the bowl with enough cold water to cover the vegetables or herbs. Using your hands, gently swish the food through the water to remove any sand or grit. Lift out the cleaned vegetables or herbs and place them in a colander to drain well. Then arrange them between layers of paper towels or clean kitchen towels to dry.

To wash them using a *salad spinner,* see the Garden Salad instructions on page 103.

Pans

Pans are an important part of cooking. Here are a few things you need to know in order to cook with them.

Measuring Pans. Be sure your pans are the kind and size specified in the recipe. This is how to take measurements on different types of pans.

◆ The size of some cookware, such as casseroles, is expressed in liquid measure at the cookware's full capacity—for instance, a 1½-quart casserole or baking dish.

◆ A baking or roasting pan is measured from the top inside for length, width, or diameter; a perpendicular measurement is taken inside for depth.

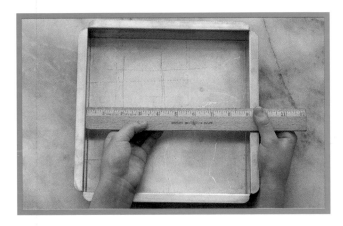

◆ Skillets are measured from the top outside for the diameter; handles are *not* included in the dimensions.

Preparing a Pan for Use. Before you begin to fry or bake, you have to prepare the pan according to the recipe's directions. Because cooked food can stick to the bottom of the pan, several recipes tell you to grease the pan before putting in the food to be fried or baked.

When greasing a pan, you can use a variety of fats.

◆ To use a *nonstick cooking spray,* spray an even layer of the oil on the bottom and sides of the pan.

◆ To use *shortening,* put a small amount on a piece of waxed paper or a paper towel and rub it in a thin, even layer on the bottom and sides of the pan.

◆ To use *butter or margarine,* cut off a small piece from the stick and apply it to the pan the way you apply the shortening. *Or* cut off a small piece from the stick, melt it in a small saucepan on top of the stove over a low heat, and then apply the melted butter or margarine to the pan with a pastry brush (see photographs on page 153).

When preparing muffins, you can grease the muffin cups with any of the fats mentioned above or save some calories by using paper or foil cupcake liners.

Sealing with Aluminum Foil

You will notice that some recipes tell you to seal food or a baking pan with a piece of aluminum foil. Here are instructions for the various sealing techniques you will be using.

◆ To seal *food,* tear off the length of aluminum foil indicated in the recipe, and place it on the cutting board. Place the food on the foil. Fold the foil up and over the food. Fold the edges of the foil over a few times to form a packet and seal the food inside.

◆ To seal a *baking pan,* tear off a length of aluminum foil that is about 3 inches longer than the length of the pan. Place the foil over the pan, and fold the edges of the foil over the edge of the pan to seal it tightly.

Preparing the Oven for Use

When you are preparing to cook a recipe in the oven, there are a few things you should do before putting the food inside to bake or roast.

1. Open the oven door to make sure there is nothing stored inside, such as pans. If so, remove them.

2. Put the baking pan you will be using in the oven to make sure that it fits.

3. Look at the two racks in the oven. They can be adjusted up and down. They can also slide in and out of the oven. This makes it easier and safer to put food into a hot oven and to remove hot food from it. In this cookbook, all the baking and roasting is done on a rack placed in the middle of the oven. If the racks in your oven are not arranged in this way, rearrange them now. Place the remaining rack above or below the rack in the middle of the oven.

4. Put the oven thermometer in the oven on the rack where the food will be placed. Because the internal temperature of different ovens can vary as much as 25° F above or below the temperature set on the oven dial, it is wise to use an oven thermometer. That way you will know for certain when the correct temperature is reached.

5. Close the oven door.

6. Set the oven control to the temperature called for in the recipe. Set the timer, allowing 10 minutes for the oven to preheat—or to reach the temperature you have set.

7. When the timer goes off, read the oven thermometer to see if the desired temperature has been reached. If it hasn't, close the oven door, adjust the temperature control up or down, and set the timer for 10 minutes. When the timer goes off, read the oven thermometer again to see that the desired temperature has been reached. If the oven is too hot, turn it off and let it cool for 10 minutes. Then set the oven temperature to slightly lower and check again.

8. When you are ready to place the food in the oven, open the oven door and, using pot holders, slide out the oven rack. Quickly place the baking pan in the center of the rack (not near an oven wall) and gently slide the rack back into the oven. Close the oven door. Set the timer and proceed with the recipe.

9. Remember to close the oven door as soon as you take something out of the oven. Otherwise hot air will escape and the oven temperature will go down, lengthening the cooking time.

10. When you are finished with the recipe, be sure to turn off the oven.

TESTING FOR DONENESS

Food must be thoroughly cooked in order to kill harmful bacteria that can cause illness. This section tells you how to determine when a food is cooked fully.

Meats

Pan-Fried. To test such pan-fried meat as pork chops and such ground meat mixtures as meatballs and patties for doneness:

Turn off the heat. Using a pot holder, carefully remove the skillet from the stove and place it on a trivet. Hold the handle of the skillet with the pot holder.

If you are pan-frying *patties,* use a pancake turner to put the patties on a clean plate. If you are pan-frying *pork chops,* use tongs to put the pork chops on a clean plate.

Using a paring knife, cut into the pieces of meat to see if they have lost their pink color

throughout. If some pieces haven't, put them back into the skillet. Holding the handle of the skillet with the pot holder, carefully put the skillet back on the stove. Set the timer and continue cooking for 2 minutes longer over a medium heat. Then repeat this test.

Baked. To test such baked ground meat mixtures as meat loaves for doneness:

Using a pot holder, carefully remove the muffin pan from the oven and place it on a trivet. Close the oven door. Hold a side of the pan with the pot holder.

If you are *using an instant-read thermometer,* insert it into the center of one of the meat loaves. The meat loaves are done when the thermometer registers at least 165° F. If it doesn't, remove the thermometer and, using the pot holders, carefully put the pan back into the oven. Set the timer and continue baking for 10 minutes longer. Then repeat this test.

If you are *not using an instant-read thermometer,* carefully use 2 forks to lift out a meat loaf from the pan and place it on a clean plate. Using a paring knife, cut into the meat loaf to see if it has lost its pink color throughout. If it hasn't, use the 2 forks to put the meat loaf back into the pan.

Using pot holders, put the pan back into the oven. Set the timer and continue baking for 10 minutes longer. Then repeat this test.

Poultry

Pan-Fried. To test pan-fried chicken cutlets for doneness:

Turn off the heat. Using a pot holder, carefully remove the skillet from the stove and place it on a trivet. Still holding the handle of the skillet with the pot holder, use tongs to put the cutlets on a clean plate. Using a paring knife, cut into the cutlets to see if they have lost their pink color throughout. If some haven't, use the tongs to put them back into the skillet. Holding the handle of the skillet with the pot holder, careful-

ly put the skillet back on the stove. Set the timer and continue cooking for 1 minute longer over a medium heat. Then repeat this test.

Baked. To test baked chicken drumsticks for doneness:

Using pot holders, carefully remove the baking pan from the oven and place it on a trivet. Close the oven door. Holding a side of the pan with a pot holder, use tongs to put a few drumsticks on a clean plate. Using a paring knife, cut into the thickest part of the drumsticks to see if they have lost their pink color throughout and if the juices run clear. If not, use the tongs to put them back into the pan. Using the pot holders, put the pan back into the oven. Set the timer and continue baking for 10 minutes longer. Then repeat this test.

Roasted. To test roasted chicken for doneness:

Using pot holders, carefully pull out the oven rack that the roasting pan is on.

If you are using a *meat thermometer,* check to see if it registers 175° to 180° F. If it doesn't, using the pot holders, carefully push the oven rack back into the oven. Set the timer and continue roasting for 10 minutes longer. Then repeat this test to check the temperature.

If you are using an *instant-read thermometer,* use pot holders to remove the pan carefully from the oven and place it on top of the stove. Close the oven door. Holding a side of the pan with a pot holder, insert the instant-read thermometer into the thickest part of the thigh, next to the body. Be very careful that the pointed end of the thermometer does not touch the thighbone. Check to see if the thermometer registers 175° to 180° F. If it does not, remove the thermometer and, using the pot holders, carefully put the pan back into the oven. Set the timer and continue roasting for 10 minutes longer. Then repeat this test to check the temperature.

If you are *not using any thermometer,* use pot holders to remove the pan carefully from the oven and place it on top of the stove. Close the oven door. Holding a side of the pan with a pot holder, use the tip of a paring knife or a fork to pierce the chicken at the thickest part of the thigh to see if the juices run clear, not pink. As an

extra check, hold a side of the pan with a pot holder, and use tongs to lift or twist the drumstick to see if it moves easily in its socket. If it doesn't, using the pot holders, carefully put the pan back into the oven. Set the timer and continue roasting for 10 minutes longer. Then repeat this test.

Fish

Baked. To test baked fish fillets for doneness:

Using pot holders, carefully remove the cookie sheet from the oven and place it on a trivet. Close the oven door. Set the timer and let the packets cool for 3 minutes. When the timer goes off, use the pot holders and tongs to open a packet carefully. *Make sure that you start from the side that is farthest away from you.* This will allow the trapped steam to escape. Using a clean fork, pierce the fish to see if it flakes easily. Use the pot holders to reseal the packet if it doesn't. Still using the pot holders, put the cookie sheet back into the oven. Set the timer and continue baking for 2 to 3 minutes longer. Then repeat this test.

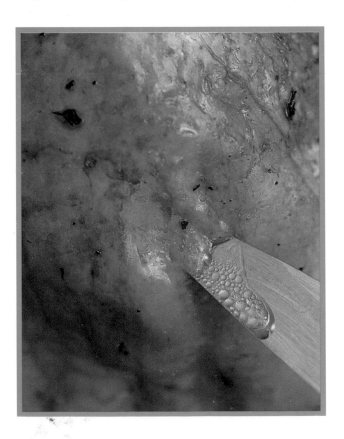

Potatoes and Other Vegetables

Boiled. To test boiled potatoes and other vegetables for doneness:

Turn off the heat. Holding the handle of the saucepan with a pot holder, use a slotted spoon to put a piece of vegetable or a potato carefully on a small plate. Using a clean fork, pierce the vegetable or potato to see if it feels soft and tender. If it doesn't, use the slotted spoon to put the vegetable or potato back into the saucepan. Set the timer and continue cooking for 2 minutes longer over a medium heat. Then repeat this test.

Baked in a Jelly-roll Pan. To test potatoes that are baked in a jelly-roll pan for doneness:

Using pot holders, carefully remove the pan from the oven and place it on top of the stove. Close the oven door. Holding a side of the pan with a pot holder, use a clean fork to put a potato on a small plate. Still using the fork, pierce the potato to see if it feels soft and tender. If it doesn't, use the fork to put the potato back into the pan. Using the pot holders, carefully put the pan back into the oven. Set the timer and continue baking for 5 minutes longer. Then repeat this test.

Baked in a Casserole. To test vegetables that are baked in a casserole for doneness:

Using pot holders, carefully remove the casserole from the oven and place it on a trivet. Close the oven door.

If the casserole is covered with a *lid,* use a pot holder to remove the lid carefully and place it on the table or work surface. If the casserole is covered with *aluminum foil,* hold a side of the casserole with a pot holder and use another pot holder to pull off the foil carefully, *starting from the area that is farthest away from you.* This will allow the trapped steam to escape.

Still holding a side of the casserole with a pot holder, use a paring knife to pierce the vegetables to the bottom layer to see if all the vegetables feel soft. If they don't, using the pot holders, carefully place the lid or the foil over the casserole again. Still using the pot holders, carefully

put the casserole back into the oven. Set the timer and continue baking for 5 minutes longer. Then repeat this test.

Pan-Fried. To test pan-fried vegetables for doneness:

Turn off the heat. Using a pot holder, carefully remove the skillet from the stove and place it on a trivet. Use a slotted spoon to put some vegetables carefully on a small plate. Set the timer and let them cool for 3 minutes. Using a clean fork, taste the vegetables to see if they are cooked to the amount of softness indicated in the recipe. If they aren't, use the slotted spoon to put them back into the skillet. Holding the handle of the skillet with the pot holder, carefully put the skillet back on the stove. Set the timer and continue cooking for 2 minutes longer over a medium heat. Then repeat this test.

Pasta

Boiled. To test boiled pasta for doneness:

Turn off the heat. Holding the handle of the saucepot with a pot holder, use a slotted spoon to remove a piece of pasta carefully. Rinse the pasta with running cold water to cool it well. Using a clean fork, taste the pasta to see if it is al dente—or slightly firm. If it isn't, set the timer and continue cooking for 2 minutes longer over a medium heat. Then repeat this test.

Baked Goods

Baked in a Muffin, Loaf, or Baking Pan. To test muffins, breads, brownies, and other baked goods that are baked in a muffin, loaf, or baking pan for doneness:

Using pot holders, carefully remove the pan from the oven and place it on the cooling rack. Close the oven door. Hold a side of the pan with a pot holder.

If you are baking *such baked goods as muffins in the muffin pan,* insert a toothpick into the center of one of the baked goods and see if it comes out clean.

If you are baking *such baked goods as bread or brownies in the loaf or baking pan,* insert a wooden skewer into the center of the baked goods and see if it comes out clean.

If the toothpick or skewer comes out with some batter sticking to it, using the pot holders, carefully put the pan back into the oven. Set the timer and continue baking for 5 minutes longer. Then repeat this test.

Baked on a Cookie Sheet. To test cookies, biscuits, and other baked goods that are baked on a cookie sheet for doneness:

Using pot holders, carefully pull out the oven rack that the cookie sheet is on and see if the cookies, biscuits, or other baked goods are golden brown. If they are pale, using the pot holders, carefully push the oven rack back into the oven. Set the timer and continue baking for 3 minutes longer. Then repeat this test.

Recipes

◆ ◆ ◆ ◆ ◆ ◆ ◆ ◆ ◆ ◆ ◆ ◆ ◆

BREAKFASTS

LUNCHES

DINNERS

SNACKS, SALADS, AND SIDE DISHES

DRINKS AND DESSERTS

Breakfasts

◆ ◆ ◆ ◆ ◆ ◆ ◆ ◆ ◆ ◆ ◆ ◆

Here is a basic recipe for scrambled eggs with some variations to suit every morning personality. It can easily be doubled.

Scrumptious Scrambled Eggs

BASIC SCRAMBLED EGGS

5 minutes
PREPARATION

5 minutes
COOKING

10 minutes
TOTAL TIME

DEGREE OF DIFFICULTY: **EASY**

SERVINGS: **1**

UTENSILS
Cutting board
Measuring spoons
Small cup or bowl
Small mixing bowl
Fork or whisk
8-inch nonstick skillet
Pot holder
Wooden spoon or heat-proof plastic spatula
Trivet
Plate

INGREDIENTS
2 large eggs
2 tablespoons milk or low fat milk
    (1 percent)
Pinch of salt
Pinch of pepper
1 teaspoon butter or margarine

1. Crack the eggs into the small bowl; discard the shells.

Pour the cracked eggs, milk, salt, and pepper into the mixing bowl. With the fork, beat the mixture until it is well combined.

▲**2.** Melt the butter in the skillet on the stove over a medium heat. Pour the egg mixture into the skillet.

▲**3.** Holding the handle of the skillet with the pot holder, lift the cooked portion of the egg mixture with the wooden spoon as it begins to set, or cook, along the edges of the skillet.

4. Move the cooked eggs toward the center; this will allow the uncooked eggs to run underneath. Repeat this step until all the eggs are set but still moist.

▲**5.** When the eggs are cooked, turn off the heat. Holding the handle of the skillet with the pot holder, place the skillet on the trivet. Spoon the scrambled eggs onto a plate.

HERB AND CHEESE SCRAMBLED EGGS

ADDITIONAL INGREDIENTS

1 tablespoon grated Parmesan cheese
2 teaspoons chopped fresh basil or
    ½ teaspoon dried basil leaves

1. Follow step 1 in the Basic Scrambled Eggs recipe, adding the Parmesan cheese and basil to the egg mixture.

▲**2.** Follow steps 2, 3, 4, and 5.

If you like your breakfasts a little spicy, this is the recipe for you!

Tex-Mex Eggs

10 minutes
PREPARATION

5 minutes
COOKING

15 minutes
TOTAL TIME

DEGREE OF DIFFICULTY: EASY
SERVINGS: 1

UTENSILS

Cutting board
Measuring spoons
¼-cup dry measuring cup
Paring knife
20-inch piece aluminum foil
Pot holders
Timer
Small bowl or cup
Small mixing bowl
Fork or whisk
8-inch nonstick skillet
Wooden spoon or heat-proof plastic
    spatula
Trivet
Tongs
Plate
Spoon

INGREDIENTS

1 scallion
1 flour tortilla (about 8 inches in diameter)
2 large eggs
2 tablespoons milk or low fat milk
    (1 percent)

Pinch of salt
Pinch of pepper
1 teaspoon butter or margarine
¼ cup shredded cheddar cheese
1 tablespoon mild salsa

▲ **1.** Preheat the oven to 350° F.

▲ **2.** Rinse the scallion with running cold water. Pat it dry.

Place the scallion on the cutting board. With the paring knife, cut off the roots and trim off the dark green ends. Discard the roots and ends. Cut the scallion crosswise into thin slices. Set the slices aside.

3. Place the aluminum foil on the cutting board. Place the tortilla on the foil. Fold the foil up and over the tortilla. Fold the edges of the foil over a few times to seal the packet.

mixture with the wooden spoon as it begins to set, or cook, along the edges of the skillet. Move the cooked eggs toward the center; this will allow the uncooked eggs to run underneath. Repeat this step until all the eggs are set but still moist.

While the eggs are cooking, sprinkle the cheddar cheese on top.

When the eggs are cooked, turn off the heat. Holding the handle of the skillet with a pot holder, place the skillet on the trivet.

▲**9.** Using a pot holder and the tongs, remove the foil from the tortilla and discard it. Still using the tongs, place the tortilla on a plate.

▲**10.** Holding the handle of the skillet with a pot holder, spoon the eggs down the center of the tortilla. Spoon the salsa on top of the eggs.

Fold the bottom edge of the tortilla up over the eggs about 1 inch. Fold the left and right sides of the tortilla over the eggs to cover the filling.

▲**4.** Using the pot holders, place the packet in the oven. Set the timer and bake the tortilla for 5 minutes.

5. While the tortilla is heating, crack the eggs into the small bowl; discard the shells.

Pour the cracked eggs, milk, salt, and pepper into the mixing bowl. Add the scallion. With the fork, beat the egg mixture until it is well combined.

▲**6.** When the timer for the tortilla goes off, use the pot holders to remove the foil packet carefully from the oven. Place it on the cutting board. Turn off the oven.

▲**7.** Melt the butter in the skillet on the stove over a medium heat. Pour the egg mixture into the skillet.

▲**8.** Holding the handle of the skillet with a pot holder, lift the cooked portion of the egg

Fragrant with orange and cinnamon, this French toast is partially made the night before. All you have to do when you wake up is the cooking.

Overnight French Toast

| 20 minutes | 20 minutes | 40 minutes |
| PREPARATION | COOKING | TOTAL TIME |

DEGREE OF DIFFICULTY: **EASY**
SERVINGS: **6**

UTENSILS
Cutting board
2-cup liquid measuring cup
Measuring spoons
Serrated knife
12-inch piece waxed paper
Grater
Plastic wrap
Small bowl or cup
13-inch-by-9-inch baking dish
Fork or whisk
Timer
Kitchen knife
Paper towel
Cookie sheet
Pancake turner
Pot holders
Trivet
Serving plate

INGREDIENTS
1 long loaf Italian bread (about 8 ounces)
1 large orange (about 8 ounces)
3 large eggs
1½ cups milk or low fat milk (1 percent)
2 tablespoons packed brown sugar
1½ teaspoons ground cinnamon
1 teaspoon vanilla extract
Butter or margarine

SERVING SUGGESTION
Softened butter or margarine, honey, maple syrup, or your favorite topping

▲**1.** The night before, place the loaf of bread on the cutting board. With the serrated knife, slice off the ends of the loaf of bread. Save these pieces for making bread crumbs another day. Cut the remaining loaf into 12 equal slices. Set the slices aside.

▲**2.** Wash the orange with running cold water. Pat it dry. Place the waxed paper on the cutting board. Place the grater on the waxed paper. Rub the orange along the side of the grater with the medium-size holes. *Do this slowly and carefully so that you do not scrape your knuckles.* Also, rub gently so that you remove only the orange skin, not the bitter white pith beneath it. Grate enough peel to measure 1 teaspoon. Wrap the orange in plastic wrap, and refrigerate to eat or use another day.

3. Crack the eggs into the small bowl; discard the shells. Pour the cracked eggs, milk, brown sugar, cinnamon, vanilla, and grated orange peel into the baking dish. With the fork, beat the egg mixture until it is well combined.

4. Place the bread slices in the egg mixture. Set the timer and let them soak for 1 minute. With the fork, turn each slice over.

5. Cover the baking dish with plastic wrap and refrigerate overnight.

▲**6.** In the morning, preheat the oven to 400° F.

▲**7.** With the kitchen knife, cut off a small piece of butter. Using the paper towel, rub the butter all over the cookie sheet to grease it. Discard the paper towel.

▲**8.** Using the pancake turner, place the bread slices on the cookie sheet. Using the pot holders, place the cookie sheet in the oven. Set the timer and bake the slices for 10 minutes, or until they are golden brown.

▲**9.** To see if they are golden brown, using the pot holders, remove the cookie sheet from the oven and place it on the trivet. Holding one side of the cookie sheet with a pot holder, use the pancake turner to lift up one edge and take a look.

If the bread slice is not golden brown, using the pot holders, carefully put the cookie sheet back into the oven. Set the timer and continue baking for 5 minutes longer. Then repeat this test.

When one side of the bread slice is golden brown, use the pancake turner to turn all of the slices over.

▲**10.** Using the pot holders, put the cookie sheet back in the oven. Set the timer and continue baking the bread slices for 10 minutes, or until they are golden brown and puffy. Turn off the oven.

▲**11.** Using the pot holders, remove the cookie sheet from the oven and place it on the trivet. Holding one side of the cookie sheet with a pot holder, use the pancake turner to put the French toast on a serving plate.

Serve right away with softened butter or margarine, honey, maple syrup, or your favorite topping.

Everybody loves cream cheese and jelly sandwiches, but they are even more delicious when they're grilled! This recipe can easily be doubled.

Grilled Cream Cheese and Jelly Sandwiches

15 minutes	5 minutes	20 minutes
PREPARATION	COOKING	TOTAL TIME

DEGREE OF DIFFICULTY: **EASY**

SERVINGS: **2**

UTENSILS
Cutting board
Measuring spoons
¼-cup dry measuring cup
Small cup or bowl
Pie plate
Fork
12-inch piece waxed paper
Table knife
10-inch skillet
Pancake turner
Timer
Pot holder
Trivet
Plates

INGREDIENTS
1 large egg
1 tablespoon water
¼ cup wheat germ
4 slices whole wheat bread
¼ cup whipped cream cheese or whipped light cream cheese
¼ cup strawberry all-fruit preserves
1 tablespoon butter or margarine

SERVING SUGGESTION
Maple syrup

1. Crack the egg into the small bowl; discard the shells.

Pour the cracked egg into the pie plate. Add the water. Using the fork, beat the egg and water until they are well combined.

2. Place the wheat germ on the waxed paper.

3. Place the bread slices on the cutting board. Using the table knife, divide the cream cheese in half. Spread 1 slice of bread with one-half of the cream cheese. Repeat with another slice of bread and the other half of the cream cheese.

4. Using the table knife, spread half of the preserves on each of the other 2 slices of bread. Place these slices of bread, preserve side down, on the cream cheese to make 2 sandwiches.

5. Holding each sandwich with your fingers, dip both sides of it into the egg mixture to moisten. Then dip both sides into the wheat germ to coat well.

▲**6.** Melt the butter in the skillet on the stove over a medium heat. Place each sandwich, one at a time, on the pancake turner. Using your other hand, slide each one into the skillet.

▲**7.** Set the timer and cook the sandwiches for 2 minutes, or until the bottom sides are toasted and golden. To see if the sandwiches are toasted, hold the handle of the skillet with a pot holder, lift up one corner of each sandwich with the pancake turner, and take a look.

▲**8.** Holding the handle of the skillet with the pot holder, turn the sandwiches with the pancake turner. Set the timer and cook the sandwiches for 2 minutes, or until this side is toasted and golden. Turn off the heat.

▲**9.** Holding the handle of the skillet with the pot holder, place the skillet on the trivet. Use the pancake turner to put each sandwich on a plate.

Serve right away, with maple syrup if you like.

These old favorites are updated with the addition of cornmeal and buttermilk. Bursting with blueberries, they are great for breakfast or a snack.

Blueberry Corn Muffins

25 minutes
PREPARATION

20 minutes
COOKING

45 minutes
TOTAL TIME

DEGREE OF DIFFICULTY: **EASY**
YIELD: **12 MUFFINS**

UTENSILS
Cutting board
1-cup and ½-cup dry measuring cups
Measuring spoons
1-cup liquid measuring cup
12 paper or foil cupcake liners or nonstick
    cooking spray
Muffin pan with twelve 2 ½-inch-by-1¼-
    inch cups
Colander
2 large mixing bowls
Wooden spoon
Small bowl or cup
Fork or whisk
Rubber spatula
Tablespoon
Pot holders
Timer
Toothpick
Cooling rack
Table knife

INGREDIENTS
1 cup fresh or frozen blueberries
    (do not thaw)
1 cup all-purpose flour
1 cup yellow cornmeal
½ cup sugar
1 teaspoon baking powder
½ teaspoon baking soda
½ teaspoon salt
1 large egg
1 cup buttermilk
¼ cup vegetable oil

SERVING SUGGESTION
Butter, jam, or cream cheese

▲ **1.** Preheat the oven to 400° F.

2. Place a cupcake liner in each muffin cup, or spray each cup with the nonstick cooking spray. Set the muffin pan aside.

3. If you are using *fresh blueberries,* place them in the colander. Pick out and discard any stems and any shriveled berries. Rinse the blueberries under running cold water and allow them to drain.

If you are using *frozen blueberries,* do not thaw them. Measure them out and keep them in the freezer until you need them in step 7.

4. Pour the flour, cornmeal, sugar, baking powder, baking soda, and salt into one of the mixing bowls. With the wooden spoon, stir the flour mixture until it is well combined.

5. Crack the egg into the small bowl; discard the shells.

Pour the cracked egg, buttermilk, and vegetable oil into the other mixing bowl. With the fork, beat the buttermilk mixture until it is well combined.

6. With the wooden spoon, stir the buttermilk mixture into the flour mixture until it is just moistened. Do not mix the batter too much; it should be lumpy.

7. Using the spatula, gently fold the fresh or frozen blueberries into the batter; be careful not to mash them.

8. Using the tablespoon, fill each muffin cup with batter about three-quarters full. Using the spatula, scrape up all the batter from the mixing bowl and add it to the muffin cups. If you spilled any batter on the muffin pan, wipe it off with a damp sponge.

▲**9.** Using the pot holders, place the muffin pan in the oven. Set the timer and bake the muffins for 18 minutes.

When the timer goes off, begin testing the muffins for doneness by inserting the toothpick into the center of one of them to see if it comes out clean (see pages 21–22 for complete instructions). When the muffins are fully baked, turn off the oven.

Set the timer and let the muffins cool for 5 minutes.

▲**10.** Holding a side of the muffin pan with a pot holder, run the table knife around the edge of each muffin to loosen it from the pan. Still using the pot holders, turn over the muffin pan and let the muffins fall out onto the cooling rack. Turn the muffins right side up and let them cool for about 15 minutes. Serve the Blueberry Corn Muffins warm or at room temperature.

HINT: If you can't find buttermilk, make your own. Put 1 tablespoon of white vinegar or lemon juice in a 1-cup liquid measuring cup. Fill the cup with milk to the 1-cup line and stir with a spoon.

Not a sweet snack, but a deliciously healthy way to start the day.

Morning Glory Muffins

 25 minutes
PREPARATION

 20 minutes
COOKING

 45 minutes
TOTAL TIME

DEGREE OF DIFFICULTY: **EASY**
YIELD: **12 MUFFINS**

UTENSILS
Cutting board
1-cup, ¼-cup, and ½-cup dry
    measuring cups
Measuring spoons
1-cup liquid measuring cup
12 paper or foil cupcake liners or
    nonstick cooking spray
Muffin pan with twelve 2 ½-inch-by-1¼-
    inch cups
Vegetable peeler
Paring knife
Grater
3 large mixing bowls
12-inch piece waxed paper
Plastic wrap
Wooden spoon
Small bowl or cup
Fork or whisk
Rubber spatula
Tablespoon
Pot holders
Timer
Cooling rack
Toothpick
Table knife

INGREDIENTS
4 carrots (about 6 ounces)
1 orange (about 8 ounces)
1¼ cups whole wheat flour
½ cup all-purpose flour
¼ cup wheat germ
1 teaspoon baking soda
1 teaspoon baking powder
1 teaspoon ground cinnamon
2 large eggs
1 container plain low fat yogurt (8-ounce
    size)
½ cup honey
3 tablespoons vegetable oil
½ cup raisins

SERVING SUGGESTION
Cream cheese, jelly, or jam

▲**1.** Preheat the oven to 350° F.

2. Place a cupcake liner in each muffin cup, or spray each cup with the nonstick cooking spray. Set the muffin pan aside.

▲**3.** Place the carrots on the cutting board. Using the vegetable peeler, peel off the skins.

With the paring knife, cut off the ends. Discard the skins and ends.

Place the grater in one of the mixing bowls. Rub each carrot along the side of the grater with the largest holes. *Do this slowly and carefully so that you do not scrape your knuckles. Stop when the carrot gets too small to hold.* You should have 1 cup of shredded carrot.

▲**4.** Wash the orange with running cold water. Pat it dry.

Place the waxed paper on the cutting board. Place the grater on the waxed paper. Rub the orange along the side of the grater with the medium-size holes. *Do this slowly and carefully so that you do not scrape your knuckles.* Also, rub gently so that you remove only the orange skin, not the bitter white pith beneath it. Grate enough peel to measure 1 teaspoon. Wrap the orange in plastic wrap and refrigerate to eat or use another day.

5. Pour the whole wheat flour, all-purpose flour, wheat germ, baking soda, baking powder, and ground cinnamon into the second mixing bowl. With the wooden spoon, stir the flour mixture until it is well combined.

6. Crack the eggs into the small bowl; discard the shells.

Pour the cracked eggs, yogurt, honey, vegetable oil, and grated orange peel into the third mixing bowl. With the fork, stir the yogurt mixture until it is well combined.

7. With the wooden spoon, stir the yogurt mixture into the flour mixture until it is just moistened. Do not mix the batter too much; it should be lumpy.

Using the spatula, fold the carrots and raisins into the batter.

8. Using the tablespoon, fill each muffin cup with batter about three-quarters full. Using the spatula, scrape up all the batter from the mixing bowl and add it to the muffin cups. If you spill any batter on the muffin pan, wipe it off with a damp sponge.

▲**9.** Using the pot holders, place the muffin pan in the oven. Set the timer and bake the muffins for 18 minutes.

When the timer goes off, begin testing the muffins for doneness by inserting the toothpick into the center of one of them to see if it comes out clean (see pages 21–22 for complete instructions). When the muffins are fully baked, turn off the oven.

10. Set the timer and let the muffins cool for 5 minutes.

▲**11.** Holding a side of the muffin pan with a pot holder, run the table knife around the edge of each muffin to loosen it from the pan. Still using the pot holders, turn over the muffin pan and let the muffins fall out onto the cooling rack. Turn the muffins right side up and let them cool for about 15 minutes.

Serve the Morning Glory Muffins warm or at room temperature. Spread them with cream cheese or your favorite jelly or jam.

ere are two ways to turn ordinary toast into something extraordinary.

Toast Toppers

FRUITED COTTAGE CHEESE

15 minutes
PREPARATION

0 minutes
COOKING

15 minutes
TOTAL TIME

DEGREE OF DIFFICULTY: **EASY**
YIELD: ³/₄ **CUP**

UTENSILS
Cutting board
¼-cup and ½-cup dry measuring cups
Measuring spoons
Paring knife
Blender
Timer
Rubber spatula
Small mixing bowl
Wooden spoon

INGREDIENTS
¼ cup dried fruits (such as apples, pears, apricots, peaches, pitted prunes)
½ cup cottage cheese or low fat cottage cheese (1 percent)
1 tablespoon milk or low fat milk (1 percent)
⅛ teaspoon ground cinnamon
2 tablespoons raisins

SERVING SUGGESTION
Toast, English muffins, or bagels

▲**1.** Place the dried fruits on the cutting board. With the paring knife, dice each piece of fruit; set the fruits aside.

2. Put the cottage cheese, milk, and ground cinnamon in the blender container. Press the lid of the blender firmly into place. Set the timer and blend the mixture on medium speed for 30 seconds.

▲**3.** Turn off the blender. *Wait until the blender blades have completely stopped; then remove the lid.* Using the spatula, scrape down the sides of the blender container. Replace the lid. Set the timer and blend the mixture on medium speed for 30 seconds, or until it is smooth.

▲**4.** Turn off the blender. *Wait until the blender blades have completely stopped; then remove the lid.* Using the spatula, scrape the mixture into the mixing bowl.

5. With the wooden spoon, stir in the raisins and dried fruits.

Serve the Fruited Cottage Cheese on warm toast, English muffins, or bagels.

Refrigerate any leftovers in a food storage container and use within 1 week.

PEACH BUTTER

10 minutes
PREPARATION

15 minutes
COOKING

25 minutes
TOTAL TIME

DEGREE OF DIFFICULTY: **EASY**
YIELD: **1 ¼ CUPS**

UTENSILS
Cutting board
1-cup and ¼-cup dry measuring cups
1-cup liquid measuring cup
1-quart saucepan with lid
Timer
Pot holder
Wooden spoon
Trivet
Food processor with knife blade
    attached
Rubber spatula

INGREDIENTS
1 cup dried peaches
1 cup orange juice
¼ cup sugar

▲**1.** Put the dried peaches, orange juice, and sugar in the saucepan. Bring the mixture to a boil on the stove over a high heat.

▲**2.** Turn down the heat to low. Cover the saucepan with the lid. Set the timer and cook the mixture for 10 minutes.

▲**3.** Using the pot holder, remove the lid and put it in the sink. Holding the handle of the saucepan with the pot holder, stir the mixture with the wooden spoon. Set the timer and continue cooking the mixture for 5 minutes over a low heat. Turn off the heat.

▲**4.** Holding the handle of the saucepan with the pot holder, place the saucepan on the trivet.

▲**5.** Holding the handle of the saucepan with the pot holder, use the wooden spoon to put the peach mixture into the food processor. Put on the lid. Set the timer and process the mixture for 1 minute.

▲**6.** Using the spatula, scrape down the side of the food processor bowl. Replace the lid. Set the timer and process the mixture for 1 minute, or until it is smooth.

Serve the Peach Butter on warm toast, English muffins, muffins, or scones.

Refrigerate any leftovers in a food storage container and use within 2 weeks.

A great way to chase the morning blues away! If your mornings are hectic, prepare the fruits (except the banana) the night before, put them in a food storage container, and refrigerate.

Breakfast Sundae

15 minutes
PREPARATION

0 minutes
COOKING

15 minutes
TOTAL TIME

DEGREE OF DIFFICULTY: **EASY**
SERVINGS: **1**

UTENSILS
Cutting board
¼-cup and ½-cup dry measuring cups
Measuring spoons
Paring knife
Melon baller
Spoon
Sundae or parfait glass

INGREDIENTS
Assorted fruits (apples, apricots, bananas,
   cherries, seedless grapes, melons,
   oranges, peaches, pears, strawberries)
1 container of your favorite low fat fruit
   yogurt (8-ounce size)or 1 cup cottage
   cheese or low fat cottage cheese (1 percent)
¼ cup of your favorite cold cereal
1 tablespoon nuts (such as sliced or
   slivered almonds, pecans, walnuts)
1 tablespoon raisins

▲**1.** Wash the fruits you have chosen with running cold water and pat them dry. Place them on the cutting board.

If you are using *apples, apricots, cherries, peaches, pears, or plums,* cut the fruits in half with the paring knife. Remove the seeds and cores with the melon baller and discard. Remove the pits with your fingers and discard.

If you are using *bananas, melons, or oranges,* remove and discard the peels or rinds. If you are using *strawberries,* remove and discard the stems.

With the paring knife, dice enough fruit to measure ½ cup.

2. Using the spoon, put half the yogurt into the glass. Next spoon half the fruit on top of the yogurt. Then spoon half the cereal on top of the fruit. Repeat this step with the remaining yogurt, fruit, and cereal.

Place the nuts on the cutting board. Break them into a few pieces with your fingers. Sprinkle the nuts and raisins on top.

Who says oatmeal is boring? When prepared with fruit, juice, and spices, it's the perfect start to a school day.

Ultimate Oatmeal

15 minutes
PREPARATION

10 minutes
COOKING

25 minutes
TOTAL TIME

DEGREE OF DIFFICULTY: **EASY**
SERVINGS: **4**

UTENSILS
Cutting board
2-cup liquid measuring cup
1-cup, ⅓-cup, and ¼-cup dry measuring cups
Measuring spoons
Paring knife
Melon baller
2-quart saucepan with lid
Pot holder
Wooden spoon
Timer
Trivet
Bowls

INGREDIENTS
1 red cooking apple, such as McIntosh
   or Rome Beauty, or 1 pear (about 6
   ounces)
1⅓ cups apple juice
1⅓ cups water
¼ cup raisins
½ teaspoon ground cinnamon
¼ teaspoon salt
1⅓ cups quick-cooking oats, uncooked

SERVING SUGGESTION
Milk and/or brown sugar

▲1. Rinse the apple with running cold water. Pat it dry. Place the apple on the cutting board. With the paring knife, cut it in half lengthwise, starting at the stem end.

With the melon baller, scoop out and discard the seeds and core.

Place each half, flat side down, on the cutting board. With the paring knife, dice each half.

▲2. Put the apple, apple juice, water, raisins, cinnamon, and salt in the saucepan. Bring the mixture to a boil on the stove over a high heat.

Holding the handle of the saucepan with the pot holder, add the oats. Stir the mixture briefly with the wooden spoon so that the oats will not stick together.

▲3. Turn down the heat to medium. Set the timer and cook the mixture for 1 minute, stirring occasionally. Turn off the heat and cover the saucepan. Set the timer and let the mixture stand for 1 minute.

▲4. Holding the handle of the saucepan with the pot holder, place the saucepan on the trivet and spoon some oatmeal into each bowl.

Serve with milk and/or brown sugar.

Omelets are very versatile. Here are just a few delicious examples to prepare on weekends. Once you have the knack, let your imagination soar with filling possibilities.

Omelets

BASIC OMELET

5 minutes	5 minutes	10 minutes
PREPARATION	COOKING	TOTAL TIME

DEGREE OF DIFFICULTY: **MODERATE**

SERVINGS: 1

UTENSILS

Cutting board
Measuring spoons
Small bowl or cup
Small mixing bowl
Fork or whisk
8-inch nonstick skillet
Pot holder
Heat-proof plastic spatula
Plate

INGREDIENTS

2 large eggs
2 tablespoons milk or low fat milk
    (1 percent)
⅛ teaspoon salt
Pinch of pepper
1 teaspoon butter or margarine

1. Crack the eggs into the small bowl; discard the shells.

Pour the cracked eggs, milk, salt, and pepper into the mixing bowl. With the fork, beat the egg mixture until it is well combined. Set it aside.

▲**2.** Melt 1 teaspoon of butter in the non-stick skillet on the stove over a medium heat. Pour the egg mixture into the skillet. Cook until the egg begins to set, or cook, around the edges of the skillet.

▲**3.** Holding the handle of the skillet with the pot holder, slip the spatula underneath the cooked portion of the egg mixture and lift it. Tilt the skillet so that the uncooked egg can run underneath. Shake the skillet occasionally to keep the omelet moving freely.

▲**4.** Hold the handle of the skillet with the pot holder. Using the spatula, fold one side of the omelet over the other.

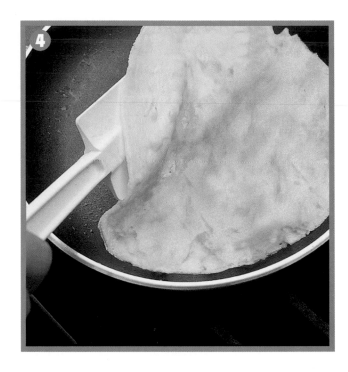

▲**5.** Tilt the skillet and slide the omelet onto a plate. Serve right away.

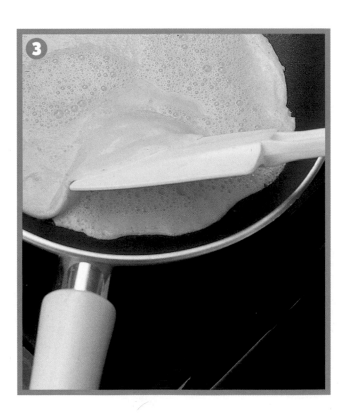

TOMATO AND MOZZARELLA OMELET

10 minutes
PREPARATION

8 minutes
COOKING

18 minutes
TOTAL TIME

ADDITIONAL UTENSILS
Paring knife
Small mixing bowl
8-inch skillet with lid
Timer
Wooden spoon
Trivet
Slotted spoon
Small plate
Fork

INGREDIENTS
1 small tomato (4 ounces)
Basic Omelet recipe ingredients
2 teaspoons butter or margarine
¼ teaspoon dried oregano leaves
¼ cup shredded mozzarella cheese

▲**1.** Rinse the tomato with running cold water. Pat it dry.

Place the tomato on the cutting board. With the paring knife, remove and discard the core. Chop the tomato. Put the pieces in the clean mixing bowl.

2. Follow step 1 in the Basic Omelet recipe.

▲**3.** Melt 2 teaspoons of butter in the skillet on the stove over a medium heat. Add the tomato pieces and oregano. Set the timer and cook the tomato for 1 minute. Holding

the handle of the skillet with the pot holder, stir the mixture occasionally with the wooden spoon.

When the timer goes off, turn off the heat and begin testing the tomato pieces for doneness by letting a piece cool for 3 minutes and then tasting it to see if it is soft and tender (see page 21 for complete instructions). When the tomato pieces are fully cooked, cover the skillet with the lid.

▲**4.** Follow steps 2 and 3.

5. When the omelet is set but still moist, spoon the tomato mixture on half of it. Sprinkle the mozzarella cheese evenly on top of the tomato mixture. Turn off the heat.

▲**6.** Follow steps 4 and 5.

MUSHROOM AND HAM OMELET

 10 minutes
PREPARATION

 10 minutes
COOKING

 20 minutes
TOTAL TIME

ADDITIONAL UTENSILS

Paring knife
Small mixing bowl
8-inch skillet with lid
Timer
Wooden spoon
Trivet
Slotted spoon
Small plate
Fork

INGREDIENTS

10 medium-size mushrooms (about ¼ pound)
2 slices cooked ham (about 1 ounce)
Basic Omelet recipe ingredients
1 tablespoon butter or margarine
½ teaspoon fresh thyme leaves or
⅛ teaspoon dried thyme leaves

▲ **1.** Rinse the mushrooms with running cold water. Pat them dry.

Place the mushrooms on the cutting board. With the paring knife, cut off and discard the end of each stem. Cut each mushroom lengthwise into thin slices. Put the slices in the clean mixing bowl.

▲ **2.** Place the ham slices one on top of the other on the cutting board. With the paring knife, cut them into thin strips. Set the slices aside.

3. Follow step 1 in the Basic Omelet recipe.

▲ **4.** Melt 1 tablespoon of butter in the skillet on top of the stove over a medium heat. Add the mushrooms, ham, and thyme. Set the timer and cook the mixture for 2 minutes. Holding the handle of the skillet with the pot holder, stir the mixture frequently with the wooden spoon.

When the timer goes off, turn off the heat and begin testing the mushrooms for doneness by letting a piece cool for 3 minutes and then tasting it to see if it is soft and tender (see page 21 for complete instructions). When the mushrooms are fully cooked, cover the skillet with the lid.

▲ **5.** Follow steps 2 and 3.

6. When the omelet is set but still moist, spoon the mushroom and ham mixture on half of it. Turn off the heat.

▲ **7.** Follow steps 4 and 5.

Lunches

◆ ◆ ◆ ◆ ◆ ◆ ◆ ◆ ◆ ◆ ◆ ◆ ◆ ◆ ◆ ◆

Surprise Burgers

Pinwheel Sandwiches

Tuna-Veggie Sandwiches

Chicken-Veggie Sandwiches

Mini Muffuletta Sandwiches

Very Vegetable Soup

Vegetarian Vegetable Soup

Chicken Rockettes

Pizza

Vegetable and Cheese Pockets

Here's a twist to an everyday hamburger. We've taken ground turkey and made it into a moist burger, then turned it inside out by putting the cheese in the middle.

Surprise Burgers

 25 minutes
PREPARATION

 15 minutes
COOKING

 40 minutes
TOTAL TIME

DEGREE OF DIFFICULTY: **EASY**
SERVINGS: **4**

UTENSILS
Cutting board
Measuring spoons
Paring knife
Grater
Large mixing bowl
Vegetable peeler
Melon baller
12-inch piece waxed paper
Small bowl or cup
Cookie sheet
12-inch skillet
Pancake turner
Pot holder
Timer
Trivet
Plate

INGREDIENTS
1 small onion (about 2 ounces)
1 small red cooking apple, such as
   McIntosh or Rome Beauty (about 5
   ounces)
1 large egg
1 pound ground turkey
½ teaspoon salt
¼ teaspoon pepper
4 slices cheddar cheese,
   2-inch-by-2-inch-by-¼-inch
1 tablespoon vegetable oil

SERVING SUGGESTION
4 English muffins, split and toasted, or 4 pita
   breads, with the top third cut off to form
   a pocket
Lettuce leaves
Tomato slices

▲ **1.** Place the onion on the cutting board. With the paring knife, cut off the ends. With the paring knife or with your fingers, peel off the skin. Discard the ends and skin.

Place the grater in the mixing bowl. Rub the onion along the side of the grater with the medium-size holes. *Do this slowly and carefully so that you do not scrape your knuckles. Stop when the onion gets too small.*

Since onions usually make the eyes tear, be careful not to put your face too close to the onion. Do not wipe your eyes with your hands if they have onion juice on them. Wash your hands before continuing with the recipe.

▲**2.** Place the apple on the cutting board. Using the vegetable peeler, peel off and discard the skin.

With the paring knife, cut the apple in half lengthwise, starting at the stem end.

With the melon baller, scoop out and discard the seeds and core.

Place the waxed paper on the cutting board. Place the grater on the waxed paper. Rub each apple half along the side of the grater with the largest holes. *Do this slowly and carefully so that you do not scrape your knuckles. Stop when each half gets too small.*

3. Crack the egg into the small bowl; discard the shells.

Put the shredded apple, cracked egg, ground turkey, salt, and pepper in the mixing bowl.

4. Using your hands, mix the ground turkey mixture until it is well combined.

Using your hands, divide the ground turkey mixture into 8 even portions. Place each portion on the cookie sheet.

Wet your hands with cold water and shape each portion of ground turkey mixture into an evenly thick patty that measures 3 ½ inches across. *Wash your hands and all*

work surfaces that have come in contact with raw ground meat before going on to any other food preparation.

5. Place a slice of cheese in the middle of each of the 4 patties. Place a plain patty on top of each cheese-covered patty. Pinch the edges of the patties together well to seal them. *Wash your hands.*

▲**6.** Heat the vegetable oil in the skillet on the stove over a medium heat. Place the patties, one at a time, on the pancake turner. Holding the handle of the skillet with the pot holder, slide each patty into the skillet.

▲**7.** Set the timer and cook the patties for 7 minutes, or until the bottom sides are lightly browned. To see if the patties are lightly browned, hold the handle of the skillet with the pot holder, lift up one patty with the washed pancake turner, and take a look.

▲**8.** Holding the handle of the skillet with the pot holder, turn the patties over with the pancake turner. Set the timer and cook the patties for 7 minutes, or until this side is lightly browned.

When the patties are lightly browned, begin testing them for doneness by cutting into them with the paring knife to see if they have lost their pink color throughout (see page 18 for complete instructions). When the patties are fully cooked, they're ready to eat.

To serve, use the pancake turner to place a Surprise Burger on each English muffin and add lettuce leaves and sliced tomatoes. Or arrange each burger in a pita bread with lettuce leaves and sliced tomatoes.

For a change of pace from the everyday sandwich, try rolling up deli meats and shredded vegetables in a flour tortilla.

Pinwheel Sandwiches

20 minutes
PREPARATION

5 minutes
COOKING

25 minutes
TOTAL TIME

DEGREE OF DIFFICULTY: **EASY**
SERVINGS: **2**

UTENSILS

Cutting board
Measuring spoons
Vegetable peeler
Paring knife
12-inch piece waxed paper
Grater
20-inch piece aluminum foil
Pot holders
Timer
Tongs
Table knife

INGREDIENTS

2 medium-size carrots (about 2 ounces each)
1 scallion
2 flour tortillas (about 8 inches in diameter)
2 tablespoons whipped cream cheese
      or whipped light cream cheese
4 slices cooked turkey
2 tablespoons cranberry-orange sauce or
      cranberry sauce

▲**1.** Preheat the oven to 350° F.

▲**2.** Place the carrots on the cutting board. Using the vegetable peeler, peel off the skins.
   With the paring knife, cut off the ends. Discard the skins and ends.
   Place the waxed paper on the cutting board. Place the grater on the waxed paper. Rub each carrot along the side of the grater with the largest holes. *Do this slowly and carefully so that you do not scrape your knuckles. Stop when the carrot gets too small to hold.*

▲**3.** Rinse the scallion under running cold water. Pat it dry.
   Place the scallion on the cutting board. With the paring knife, cut off the roots and trim off the dark green ends. Discard the roots and ends.

Cut the scallion crosswise into thin slices. Set the slices aside.

4. Place the aluminum foil on the cutting board. Place the tortillas, one on top of the other, on the foil. Fold the foil up and over the tortillas. Fold the edges of the foil over a few times to seal the packet. (See page 17.)

▲**5.** Using the pot holders, place the tortillas in the oven. Set the timer and bake them for 5 minutes.

▲**6.** Using the pot holders, remove the packet from the oven and place it on the cutting board. Turn off the oven. Using a pot holder and the tongs, remove the foil from the tortillas and discard.

7. Using the table knife, spread 1 tablespoon of cream cheese to the edges of each tortilla.

8. Sprinkle 2 tablespoons of shredded carrot and 1 tablespoon of sliced scallion on each of the tortillas.

Place 2 slices of turkey on top of each tortilla.

Spoon 1 tablespoon of cranberry-orange sauce down the center of each tortilla.

9. Starting from the edge, roll each tortilla up around the filling. If necessary, use some more cream cheese to seal it.

▲**10.** With the paring knife, cut each tortilla crosswise into 2 pieces.

Packed with lots of crunchy vegetables, this will soon become a lunch box favorite.

Tuna-Veggie Sandwiches

25 minutes
PREPARATION

0 minutes
COOKING

25 minutes
TOTAL TIME

DEGREE OF DIFFICULTY: **EASY**
SERVINGS: **4 SANDWICHES**

UTENSILS
Cutting board
⅓-cup and ½-cup dry measuring cups
Measuring spoons
Rubber spatula
Medium-size mixing bowl
Spoon
Paring knife
Vegetable peeler
Strainer
Can opener

INGREDIENTS
⅓ cup plain low fat yogurt
2 tablespoons mayonnaise or reduced fat or fat free mayonnaise
1 teaspoon prepared mustard
1 large celery stalk (about 2 ounces)
1 small red pepper (about 5 ounces)
1 small carrot (about 2 ounces)
½ cup packed spinach leaves with stems removed
1 can solid white tuna packed in water (6-ounce size)
4 mini pita breads or 8 slices whole wheat bread
4 lettuce leaves

1. Using the spatula, scrape out the yogurt and mayonnaise into the mixing bowl. Add the mustard. With the spoon, stir the mixture until it is well combined. Set the yogurt dressing aside.

2. Rinse the celery and pepper with running cold water. Pat them dry. Set the pepper aside.

▲**3.** Place the celery on the cutting board. With the paring knife, cut off and discard the ends.

Dice the celery and put the pieces in the mixing bowl.

▲**4.** Place the pepper on the cutting board. With the paring knife, cut it lengthwise in half. With the paring knife or with your fingers, remove and discard the seeds and white ribs.

With the paring knife, dice the pepper and put the pieces in the mixing bowl.

▲**5.** Place the carrot on the cutting board. Using the vegetable peeler, peel off the skin.

With the paring knife, cut off the ends. Discard the skin and ends.

Dice the carrot and put the pieces in the mixing bowl.

▲**6.** Place the spinach leaves on the cutting board, one on top of another. With the paring knife, cut them crosswise into thin strips. Put the strips in the mixing bowl.

▲**7.** Place the strainer in the sink. Using the can opener, open the can of tuna and pour the tuna into the strainer to drain off the liquid. Using the spoon, break up the tuna into large chunks. Put the tuna in the mixing bowl.

Using the spatula, gently stir the mixture until it is well combined.

▲**8.** Place the pita breads on the cutting board. With the paring knife, cut each pita crosswise in half.

9. Place a lettuce leaf in the pocket of each pita bread. Spoon some tuna-veggie salad into each pita pocket.

If you are not serving the Tuna-Veggie Sandwiches right away, wrap each sandwich tightly with plastic wrap and refrigerate. If you do not use all the mixture at one time, put it in a food storage container and refrigerate. It will keep for up to 3 days.

> **HINT:** If you are tired of sandwiches for school lunches, you can put the tuna-veggie mixture in an insulated container or a food storage container (with an ice pack to keep it cool) and take it to school. Pack some crackers or cut-up carrot and celery sticks and use them for dipping and spreading with the tuna-veggie mixture.

CHICKEN-VEGGIE SANDWICHES

As a variation, you can substitute 1½ cups of chopped cooked chicken for the canned tuna in step 7 of the Tuna-Veggie Sandwiches recipe.

Muffuletta is the name of an Italian sandwich that became popular in New Orleans in the early twentieth century.

Mini Muffuletta Sandwiches

15 minutes
PREPARATION

5 minutes
COOKING

20 minutes
TOTAL TIME

DEGREE OF DIFFICULTY: **EASY**
SERVINGS: **2**

UTENSILS
Cutting board
Measuring spoons
Medium-size mixing bowl
2 forks or 1 fork and 1 whisk
Paring knife
Vegetable peeler
Teaspoon
Spoon
Serrated knife
10-inch skillet
Pot holder
Tongs
Timer
Trivet
Plate

INGREDIENTS
1 tablespoon red wine vinegar
1 tablespoon chopped fresh dill or
    1 teaspoon dried dillweed
½ teaspoon Dijon mustard
3 tablespoons olive oil
½ teaspoon salt
6 pitted large ripe olives
½ large cucumber (about 6 ounces)
6 to 8 medium-size cherry tomatoes
    (about ¼ pound)
2 kaiser rolls
2 chicken cutlets (about 4 ounces each)

1. Put the vinegar, dill, Dijon mustard, 2 tablespoons of olive oil, and ¼ teaspoon of salt into the mixing bowl. With a fork or a whisk, beat the mixture until it is well combined. Set the salad dressing aside.

▲**2.** Place the olives on the cutting board. With the paring knife, cut each one crosswise into rings. Place the olive rings in the mixing bowl.

▲**3.** Place the cucumber on the cutting board. Using the vegetable peeler, peel off and discard the skin.

With the paring knife, cut the cucumber lengthwise in half.

With the teaspoon, scoop out and discard the seeds.

Place each half, flat side down, on the cutting board. With the paring knife, cut each half crosswise into thin slices. Put the slices in the mixing bowl.

▲**4.** Remove and discard any stems from the cherry tomatoes. Rinse the tomatoes with running cold water. Pat them dry.

Place the tomatoes on the cutting board. With the paring knife, cut each one lengthwise in half, starting at the stem end. Place each half, flat side down, on the cutting board. Cut each half in half again to make 4 quarters. Put the tomatoes in the bowl.

With the spoon, stir the mixture until it is well combined. Set the cucumber salad aside.

▲**5.** With the serrated knife, slice each roll horizontally to cut off the top third. Set the top of each roll aside. Using your fingertips, remove some of each roll's soft white center. Leave a bread shell with ½-inch-thick sides.

6. Sprinkle each chicken cutlet with ⅛ teaspoon salt. *Wash your hands and all work surfaces that have come in contact with raw chicken before going on to any other food preparation.*

▲**7.** Heat 1 tablespoon of olive oil in the skillet on the stove over a medium heat.

Holding the handle of the skillet with the pot holder, use the tongs to place the cutlets gently in the skillet.

Set the timer and cook the cutlets for 2 minutes, or until they are golden brown. To see if they are golden brown, hold the handle of the skillet with the pot holder, lift up one end of each cutlet with the washed tongs, and take a look.

▲**8.** Holding the handle of the skillet with the pot holder, turn the cutlets over with the tongs. Set the timer and cook the cutlets for 2 minutes, or until this side is golden brown.

When the cutlets are golden brown, begin testing them for doneness by cutting into them with the paring knife to see if they have lost their pink color throughout (see page 19 for complete instructions). When they are fully cooked, put them on the cutting board, using the tongs.

▲**9.** Holding each cutlet with a clean fork, cut it crosswise in half with the paring knife.

10. Spoon some cucumber salad into the bottom part of each roll. Put two chicken halves on top of the salad. Spoon more salad on top of the chicken. Replace the top of each roll.

If this is going to be your lunch tomorrow, wrap each sandwich tightly with plastic wrap and refrigerate overnight.

A hearty and delicious soup that doesn't take hours to make!

Very Vegetable Soup

15 minutes
PREPARATION

25 minutes
COOKING

40 minutes
TOTAL TIME

DEGREE OF DIFFICULTY: **EASY**
SERVINGS: **6**

UTENSILS
Cutting board
4-cup liquid measuring cup
Measuring spoons
1-cup dry measuring cup
Vegetable peeler
Paring knife
Medium-size mixing bowl
Vegetable brush
Can opener
3-quart saucepan
Food storage container
Pot holders
Wooden spoon
Timer
Strainer
2-quart saucepan
Slotted spoon
Fork
Colander

INGREDIENTS
1 medium-size carrot (about 2½ ounces)
1 small yellow straightneck squash
   (about 4 ounces)
1 small zucchini (about 4 ounces)
2 cans beef or chicken broth
   (13¾- to 14½-ounce size)
3 cups low sodium vegetable juice
¼ teaspoon dried thyme leaves
1 can red kidney beans (15- to 19-ounce size)
1 cup small shell or alphabet macaroni

▲**1.** Place the carrot on the cutting board. Using the vegetable peeler, peel off the skin.
   With the paring knife, cut off the ends. Discard the skin and ends.
   Cut the carrot lengthwise in half. Place each half, flat side down, on the cutting board. Cut each half crosswise into thin slices. Put the slices in the mixing bowl.

2. With the vegetable brush, scrub the squash and zucchini while rinsing them under running cold water. Pat them dry. Set the zucchini aside.

▲3. Place the squash on the cutting board. With the paring knife, cut off and discard the ends.

Cut the squash lengthwise in half. Place each half, flat side down, on the cutting board. Cut each half lengthwise in half again to make 4 quarters.

Place the quarters, flat side down, on the cutting board. Cut each quarter crosswise into ¼-inch pieces. Put the pieces in the mixing bowl.

▲4. Place the zucchini on the cutting board. With the paring knife, cut off and discard the ends.

Cut the zucchini lengthwise in half. Place each half, flat side down, on the cutting board. Cut each half lengthwise in half again to make 4 quarters.

Place the quarters, flat side down, on the cutting board. Cut each quarter crosswise into ¼-inch pieces. Put the pieces in the mixing bowl.

▲5. Open the can of broth. Using the liquid measuring cup, pour enough broth to measure 2⅔ cups. Pour the broth into the 3-quart saucepan. Pour the leftover broth into the food storage container and refrigerate it to use another day.

Pour the vegetable juice into the saucepan. Bring the mixture to a boil on the stove over a high heat.

▲6. Add the vegetables and thyme. Holding the handle of the saucepan with a pot holder, stir the mixture with the wooden spoon.

When the mixture begins to boil again, turn down the heat to low. Set the timer and simmer the mixture for 15 minutes.

7. While the soup mixture is simmering, place the strainer in the sink. Using the can opener, open the can of kidney beans. Pour the beans into the strainer and rinse them with running cold water. Set the beans aside.

▲8. Using the 2-quart saucepan, prepare the macaroni as the package instructions direct.

When it is time to test the macaroni for doneness, rinse a piece under running cold water to cool it well and then taste it to see if it is al dente (see page 21 for complete instructions).

When the macaroni is fully cooked, turn off the heat. Place the colander in the sink. Have an adult pour the macaroni into the colander to drain the water well. *Boiling water is dangerous. Do not pour the cooked macaroni into the colander yourself.*

▲9. When the timer for the soup mixture goes off, hold the handles of the colander with the pot holders and pour the macaroni into the saucepan. Add the kidney beans. Holding the handle of the saucepan with a pot holder, stir the mixture with the wooden spoon. Set the timer and cook it for 5 minutes, or until it is hot.

Serve the Very Vegetable Soup right away, with crackers or crusty bread.

VEGETARIAN VEGETABLE SOUP

To make this soup completely vegetarian, substitute 2 cans of vegetable broth (14½-ounce size) for the beef or chicken broth in step 5 of the Very Vegetable Soup recipe.

This recipe requires a little advance planning because you marinate and bake it the night before. You can serve it hot for dinner, or eat it cold for lunch. Either way, it's great!

Chicken Rockettes

| 1 hour | 15 minutes | 55 minutes |
| MARINATING | PREPARATION | COOKING |

2 hours 10 minutes
TOTAL TIME

DEGREE OF DIFFICULTY: **MODERATE**
SERVINGS: **4**

UTENSILS

Cutting board
1-cup liquid measuring cup
Measuring spoons
Paper towels
Paring knife
Small mixing bowl
Spoon
Gallon-size sealable food storage bag
Timer
13-inch-by-9-inch baking pan
Aluminum foil
Pot holders
Trivet
Pastry brush

Tongs
Plate

INGREDIENTS

8 large chicken drumsticks (about 2½ pounds)
2 scallions
¼ cup low sodium soy sauce
2 tablespoons rice wine vinegar or white vinegar
1 tablespoon vegetable oil
1 teaspoon packed brown sugar
1 teaspoon ground ginger
Nonstick cooking spray

1. Rinse the chicken drumsticks with running cold water. Pat them dry with paper towels and discard the towels.

Grasp the skin at the wide end of each drumstick and pull it down toward the narrow end. Pull off and discard the skin. Use a paper towel to help you grip the skin better. *Wash your hands and all work surfaces that have come in contact with raw chicken before going on to any other food preparation.*

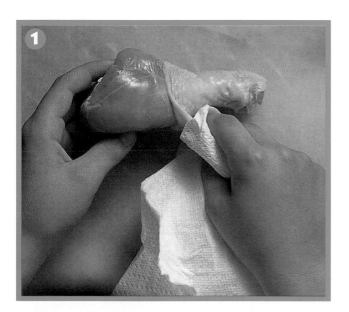

▲**2.** Rinse the scallions with running cold water. Pat them dry.

Place the scallions on the cutting board. With the paring knife, cut off the roots and trim off the dark green ends. Discard the roots and ends.

Cut each scallion crosswise into thin slices. Put the slices in the mixing bowl.

3. Pour the soy sauce, rice wine vinegar, and vegetable oil into the mixing bowl. Add the brown sugar and ginger. Stir the mixture with the spoon until the brown sugar dissolves.

4. Pour the mixture into the food storage bag. Add the drumsticks. Carefully press out some of the air and seal the bag. Turn the bag a few times, making sure that the drumsticks are coated with the soy sauce mixture.

5. Place the bag in the refrigerator. Set the timer for 30 minutes to allow the drumsticks to marinate. Turn over the bag when the timer goes off. Set the timer for 30 minutes to allow the drumsticks to continue marinating.

▲**6.** Preheat the oven to 375° F.

7. Lightly spray the baking pan with non-stick cooking spray. Put the drumsticks and the soy sauce mixture in the pan. Discard the food storage bag.

8. Tear off a piece of aluminum foil. Place the foil over the baking pan and fold the edges of the foil over the edge of the pan to seal it.

▲**9.** Using the pot holders, place the baking pan in the oven. Set the timer and bake the drumsticks for 40 minutes.

▲**10.** Using the pot holders, remove the baking pan from the oven and place it on the trivet. Pull off the foil, *starting from the corner that is farthest away from you.* This will allow the trapped steam to escape. Discard the foil.

▲**11.** Using the pastry brush, brush the drumsticks with the soy sauce mixture. Using the pot holders, put the uncovered baking pan back in the oven.

▲**12.** Set the timer and continue baking the drumsticks for 15 minutes.

When the timer goes off, begin testing the drumsticks for doneness by cutting into the thickest part with the paring knife to see if the chicken has lost its pink color throughout and the juices run clear(see page 19 for complete instructions). When they are fully baked, turn off the oven.

▲**13.** Using a pot holder, hold one side of the baking pan. Using the pastry brush, brush the drumsticks with the remaining soy sauce mixture.

If this is going to be your lunch tomorrow, place the drumsticks in a food storage container and refrigerate.

Pizza! What fun pizza making can be when you choose your own toppings.

Pizza

20 minutes
PREPARATION

40 minutes
COOKING

1 hour
TOTAL TIME

DEGREE OF DIFFICULTY: **MODERATE**
SERVINGS: **8**

UTENSILS

Cutting board
¼-cup and 1-cup dry measuring cups
2-cup liquid measuring cup
Measuring spoons
Paring knife
2-quart saucepan
Timer
12-inch-round pizza pan or 15½-inch-by-
    10½-inch jelly-roll pan
Pastry brush
Pot holders
Trivet
Ladle or large spoon
Pizza wheel or kitchen shears

INGREDIENTS

Toppings

1 green pepper or ¼ pound mushrooms or
    ¼ cup pitted large ripe olives, drained,
    or 1 ounce sliced pepperoni

Pizza

2 cups Basic Tomato Sauce (see recipe on
    pages 82–83)
1 teaspoon olive oil
1 tablespoon yellow cornmeal
1 container refrigerated all-ready pizza crust
    (10-ounce size)
2 cups shredded whole milk, part skim, or
    reduced fat mozzarella cheese (8 ounces)
2 tablespoons grated Parmesan cheese

1. Decide what toppings you want on your pizza. Then prepare them according to steps 2, 3, 4, and 5.

▲**2.** If you want *green pepper* on your pizza, rinse it with running cold water. Pat it dry.

Place the pepper on the cutting board. With the paring knife, cut it lengthwise in half. With the paring knife or your fingers, remove and discard the seeds and the white ribs.

With the paring knife, cut each half lengthwise into thin strips. Set the strips aside.

▲**3.** If you want *mushrooms* on your pizza, rinse them with running cold water. Pat them dry.

Place the mushrooms on the cutting board. With the paring knife, cut off and discard the end of each stem.

Cut each mushroom lengthwise into thin slices. Set the slices aside.

▲**4.** If you want *olives* on your pizza, place them on the cutting board. With the paring knife, cut each one crosswise into rings. Set the rings aside.

5. If you want *pepperoni* on your pizza, set the slices aside.

▲**6.** *To prepare the pizza,* pour the tomato sauce into the saucepan. Bring it to a boil on the stove over a high heat. Turn down the heat to low. Set the timer and simmer the sauce for 15 minutes.

▲**7.** While the tomato sauce is simmering, preheat the oven to 450° F.

8. Pour the olive oil into the pizza pan. Using the pastry brush, spread it on the bottom of the pan.

Sprinkle the bottom of the pan evenly with the yellow cornmeal.

9. Open the container of pizza crust. Gently unroll the dough and place it in the pan. Using your fingertips, press and stretch the dough to fit the prepared pan, starting from the center of the dough.

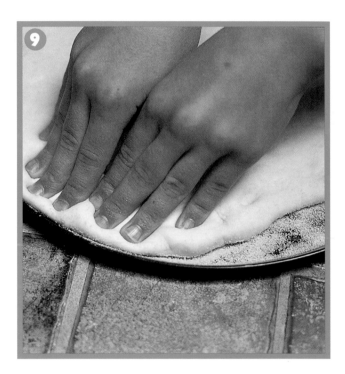

▲**10.** When the timer for the tomato sauce goes off, turn off the heat. Holding the handle of the saucepan with a pot holder, put the saucepan on the trivet. You should have about 1½ cups of tomato sauce left. Still holding the handle of the saucepan with a pot holder, use the ladle to spread the tomato sauce evenly over the dough. Stop spreading the sauce about 1 inch from the edge of the dough.

11. Sprinkle the mozzarella cheese evenly on top of the tomato sauce. Now arrange the pepper, mushrooms, olives, or pepperoni, or a combination of toppings, evenly on top of the mozzarella cheese. Then sprinkle the topping with Parmesan cheese.

▲**12.** Using the pot holders, place the pan in the oven. Set the timer and bake the pizza for 20 minutes, or until the crust is golden brown and the cheese is bubbling. Turn off the oven.

▲**13.** Using the pot holders, remove the pan from the oven and place it on the trivet. Set the timer and let the pizza cool for 5 minutes.

▲**14.** Holding the handle of the pan with a pot holder, cut the pizza into 8 portions with the pizza wheel.

OTHER TOPPING IDEAS

When you are in the mood for pizza, look in the refrigerator for possible toppings before you begin. Almost anything can go on your pizza. It's fun to mix and match toppings and to develop your own special-tasting pizza. Here are some ideas for toppings:

Cooked broccoli, yellow squash,
   or zucchini
Sliced ham
Cooked meatballs, sliced
Cooked sausage, sliced
Cooked bacon, crumbled
Cooked chicken, sliced
Fresh herbs, such as basil, oregano,
   rosemary, or thyme
Monterey Jack cheese, shredded
Cheddar cheese, shredded
American cheese, sliced
Feta cheese, crumbled

For a change of pace, here is a recipe that does not contain meat. Instead, cheese, beans, and yogurt provide the protein.

Vegetable and Cheese Pockets

| 25 minutes | 5 minutes | 30 minutes |
| PREPARATION | COOKING | TOTAL TIME |

DEGREE OF DIFFICULTY: **MODERATE**
SERVINGS: **2**

UTENSILS

Cutting board
¼-cup, ½-cup, and 1-cup dry
    measuring cups
Measuring spoons
Rubber spatula
2 medium-size mixing bowls
Spoon
Paring knife
Vegetable peeler
Plastic food storage bag
Strainer
Can opener
Food storage container
10-inch skillet
Timer
Pot holder
Wooden spoon
Trivet

Slotted spoon
Small plate
Fork

INGREDIENTS

¼ cup plain low fat yogurt
½ teaspoon lemon juice
⅛ teaspoon garlic salt
⅛ teaspoon onion powder
1 bunch broccoli (about 1½ pounds)
1 medium-size carrot (about 2 ounces)
1 scallion
1 can red kidney beans (15- to 19-ounce
    size)
1 tablespoon plus 1 teaspoon
    vegetable oil
¼ cup shredded Cheddar cheese
2 whole wheat pitas (about 6 inches in
    diameter)

1. Using the spatula, scrape the yogurt into one of the mixing bowls. Add the lemon juice, garlic salt, and onion powder. With the spoon, stir the mixture until it is well combined. Set the yogurt dressing aside.

▲**2.** Rinse the broccoli with running cold water. Pat it dry.

Place it on the cutting board. With the paring knife, cut off enough flowerets to measure 1½ cups. If any are large, cut them lengthwise in half. Put the flowerets in the other mixing bowl and set the bowl aside.

▲**3.** Using the vegetable peeler, peel off and discard the skin of the broccoli stem.

With the paring knife, cut the stem lengthwise in half. Place each half, flat side down, on the cutting board. Cut the halves crosswise into thin slices. Slice enough stem to measure ½ cup. Put the slices in the mixing bowl with the flowerets. Put the remaining broccoli in a plastic food storage bag and refrigerate it to use another day.

▲**4.** Place the carrot on the cutting board. Using the vegetable peeler, peel off the skin.

With the paring knife, cut off the ends. Discard the skin and ends.

Cut the carrot lengthwise in half. Place each half, flat side down, on the cutting board. Cut each half crosswise into thin slices. Put the slices in the bowl with the broccoli.

▲**5.** Rinse the scallion with running cold water. Pat it dry. Place it on the cutting board. With the paring knife, cut off the roots and trim off the dark green end.

Discard the roots and end. Cut the scallion crosswise into thin slices. Put the slices in the bowl with the other vegetables.

6. Place the strainer in the sink. Using the can opener, open the can of kidney beans. Using the spoon, fill the ½-cup measuring cup with beans. Pour the beans into the strainer and rinse them with running cold water. Set the beans aside. Put the leftover beans in a food storage container and refrigerate them to use another day.

▲**7.** Heat the vegetable oil in the skillet on the stove over a medium heat. Add the vegetable mixture. Set the timer and cook it for 4 minutes. Holding the handle of the skillet with the pot holder, stir the mixture occasionally with the wooden spoon.

When the timer goes off, turn off the heat and begin testing the vegetables for doneness by letting a piece cool for 3 minutes and then tasting it to see if it is tender-crisp (see page 21 for complete instructions).

When the vegetables are fully cooked, set the timer and let them cool for 5 minutes.

▲**8.** Holding the handle of the skillet with the pot holder, spoon the vegetable mixture into the mixing bowl with the yogurt mixture. Add the beans and cheese. Using the wooden spoon, stir the mixture until it is well combined.

▲**9.** Place the pita breads on the cutting board. With the paring knife, cut each crosswise in half. Spoon some vegetable and cheese mixture into each pita pocket.

Dinners

♦ ♦ ♦ ♦ ♦ ♦ ♦ ♦ ♦ ♦ ♦ ♦ ♦ ♦ ♦

Cornmeal gives these chicken cutlets their crunchy appeal. Served with dipping sauces, they are as much fun to eat as they are to make.

Crunchy Chicken Fingers

15 minutes
PREPARATION

10 minutes
COOKING

25 minutes
TOTAL TIME

DEGREE OF DIFFICULTY: **EASY**
SERVINGS: **4**

UTENSILS

Cutting board
½-cup, ¼-cup, and ⅓-cup dry measuring
    cups
Measuring spoons
Rubber spatula
2 small mixing bowls
2 spoons
12-inch piece waxed paper
Small bowl or cup
Pie plate
2 forks
Cookie sheet
12-inch skillet
Pot holder
Tongs
Timer
Trivet
Plate
Paring knife
Serving platter

INGREDIENTS

Mustard Dipping Sauce

¾ cup sour cream or light or fat free
    sour cream
3 tablespoons Dijon mustard
1 tablespoon honey

Crunchy Chicken Fingers

⅔ cup yellow cornmeal
1 teaspoon chili powder
½ teaspoon salt
1 large egg
1 tablespoon water
1¼ pounds chicken cutlets
2 tablespoons vegetable oil

SERVING SUGGESTION

1 cup prepared salsa

1. *To prepare the Mustard Dipping Sauce,* use the spatula to scrape the sour cream into one of the mixing bowls. Add the Dijon mustard and honey. With a spoon, stir the mixture until it is well combined. Set the Mustard Dipping Sauce aside.

2. *To prepare the Crunchy Chicken Fingers,* put the cornmeal, chili powder, and salt on the waxed paper. With the other spoon, stir the mixture until it is well combined.

3. Crack the egg into the small bowl; discard the shells.

Pour the cracked egg into the pie plate. Add the water. Beat the egg and water with one of the forks until they are well combined.

4. Holding a chicken cutlet with the fork or your fingers, dip both sides of it into the egg mixture to moisten. Let any excess egg mixture drip back into the pie plate.

Dip both sides of the cutlet into the cornmeal mixture to coat well. Place the coated cutlet on the cookie sheet.

Repeat this step with the remaining chicken cutlets. *Wash your hands and all work*

surfaces that have come in contact with raw chicken before going on to any other food preparation.

▲**5.** Heat the vegetable oil in the skillet on the stove over a medium heat.

Holding the handle of the skillet with the pot holder, use the tongs to place half the chicken cutlets gently in the skillet.

Set the timer and cook the cutlets for 2 minutes, or until they are golden brown. To see if they are golden brown, hold the handle of the skillet with the pot holder, lift up one end of each cutlet with the washed tongs, and take a look.

▲**6.** Holding the handle of the skillet with the pot holder, turn over the cutlets with the tongs. Set the timer and cook the cutlets for 2 minutes, or until this side is golden brown.

When the cutlets are golden brown, begin testing them for doneness by cutting into them with the paring knife to see if they have lost their pink color throughout (see page 19 for complete instructions).

▲**7.** When these cutlets are fully cooked, repeat steps 5 and 6 with the remaining cutlets, adding more vegetable oil to the skillet if needed. When you have finished cooking all the cutlets, turn off the heat.

▲**8.** Using the tongs, put the cutlets on the cutting board. Holding the cutlet with the other fork, cut each one crosswise into 1-inch-wide strips with the paring knife. Put the strips on the serving platter.

To serve, pour the salsa into the other mixing bowl. Serve the Crunchy Chicken Fingers with the Mustard Dipping Sauce and the salsa.

Fish that is moist and flavorful is a snap to make when it is cooked in a foil packet.

Fish in Foil Packets

25 minutes
PREPARATION

15 minutes
COOKING

40 minutes
TOTAL TIME

DEGREE OF DIFFICULTY: **EASY**
SERVINGS: **4**

UTENSILS
Cutting board
Measuring spoons
Paring knife
2 small mixing bowls
Vegetable brush
4 pieces aluminum foil, each 14 inches long
Large cookie sheet
Pot holders
Timer
Trivet
Tongs
Fork
4 dinner plates

INGREDIENTS
1 lemon
12 medium-size cherry tomatoes
    (about ½ pound)
1 small zucchini (about 4 ounces)
4 flounder, sole, red snapper, or catfish
    fillets (about 6 ounces each)

12 small fresh basil leaves or ½ teaspoon
    dried basil leaves
½ teaspoon salt

▲ **1.** Preheat the oven to 425° F.

▲ **2.** Rinse the lemon with running cold water. Pat it dry.
    Place the lemon on the cutting board. With the paring knife, cut it lengthwise in half. Place each half, flat side down, on the cutting board. Cut each half crosswise into 8 thin slices. Set the slices aside.

▲ **3.** Remove and discard any stems from the cherry tomatoes. Rinse them with running cold water. Pat them dry.

Place the tomatoes on the cutting board. With the paring knife, cut each one lengthwise in half, starting at the stem end. Place the halves in one of the mixing bowls.

▲**4.** With the vegetable brush, scrub the zucchini while rinsing it with running cold water. Place the zucchini on the cutting board. With the paring knife, cut off and discard the ends.

Cut the zucchini crosswise into ¼-inch slices. Put the slices in the other mixing bowl.

5. Place a piece of aluminum foil on the cutting board with the smaller side of the foil facing you. Fold the foil crosswise in half and then open it. Repeat this step with the other pieces of foil.

6. Place a fish fillet on the bottom half of each piece of foil along the folded side. Place 4 lemon slices on each fish fillet. Next arrange some zucchini slices on top of the lemon slices on each fish fillet. Then place 6 tomato halves on top of the zucchini slices on each fish fillet.

7. If you are using *fresh basil leaves,* tuck 3 leaves into the vegetables on each fish fillet. If you are using *dried basil leaves,* sprinkle the vegetables on each fish fillet with ⅛ teaspoon of dried basil.

Sprinkle the vegetables on each fish fillet with ⅛ teaspoon of salt.

8. Fold the top half of the aluminum foil over each fish fillet and vegetables to cover them. Fold the edges of each piece of foil over a few times to seal each packet (see page 17).

▲**9.** Place the packets on the cookie sheet. Using the pot holders, place the cookie sheet in the oven. Set the timer and bake the fish fillets for 15 minutes.

When the timer goes off, begin testing the fish fillets for doneness by piercing them with the fork to see if they flake easily (see page 20 for complete instructions). When they are fully baked, turn off the oven.

Everything you need for dinner is here in one pan.

Oven-Roasted Chicken and Vegetables

30 minutes
PREPARATION

2 hours
COOKING

2 hours 30 minutes
TOTAL TIME

DEGREE OF DIFFICULTY: **MODERATE**
SERVINGS: **6**

UTENSILS

Cutting board
Measuring spoons
17-inch-by-12-inch roasting pan
Cup or small bowl
Spoon
Vegetable peeler
Paring knife
Vegetable brush
Wooden spoon
Roasting rack
Paper towels
Meat thermometer or instant-read
    thermometer or fork and tongs
Timer
Pot holders
Trivet
Aluminum foil

INGREDIENTS

Nonstick cooking spray
½ teaspoon dried thyme leaves
½ teaspoon dried basil leaves
1¼ teaspoons salt
¾ teaspoon pepper
6 medium-size carrots (about 1 pound)
1 large onion (about 8 ounces)
6 medium-size red potatoes
    (about 1½ pounds)
1 tablespoon olive oil
1 lemon
1 roasting chicken, 6 to 6¼ pounds

1. Spray the roasting pan with the nonstick cooking spray. Set the pan aside.

2. Put the thyme, basil, 1 teaspoon of salt, and ½ teaspoon of pepper into the cup. Using the spoon, stir the mixture until it is well combined. Set the thyme mixture aside.

▲**3.** Place the carrots on the cutting board. Using the vegetable peeler, peel off the skins.

With the paring knife, cut off the ends. Discard the skins and ends.

Cut each carrot crosswise into 3 pieces. Put the pieces in the roasting pan.

▲**4.** Place the onion on the cutting board. With the paring knife, cut off the ends. With the paring knife or your fingers, peel off the skin. Discard the ends and skin.

Cut the onion lengthwise in half. Place each half, flat side down, on the cutting board. Cut each half lengthwise into 4 pieces. Put the pieces in the roasting pan. *Since onions usually make the eyes tear, be careful not to put your face too close to the onion. Do not wipe your eyes*

with your hands if they have onion juice on them. Wash your hands before continuing with the recipe.

▲**5.** Using the vegetable brush, scrub the potatoes while rinsing them under running cold water. Pat them dry.

Place the potatoes on the cutting board. With the paring knife, cut each one lengthwise in half. Place each half, flat side down, on the cutting board. Cut each half lengthwise in half again. Put the potato quarters in the roasting pan.

6. Sprinkle the vegetables with the olive oil, ¼ teaspoon of salt, and ¼ teaspoon of pepper. Using the wooden spoon, stir the vegetables until they are evenly coated with the olive oil and seasonings.

▲**7.** Rinse the lemon with running cold water. Pat it dry.

Place the lemon on the cutting board. With the paring knife, cut it crosswise in half. Set the halves aside.

8. Using the wooden spoon, push the vegetables to the sides of the roasting pan to make room for the roasting rack. Place the rack in the center of the pan.

9. Remove the package that contains the giblets and neck from inside the chicken. This package can be wrapped and refrigerated and used to make soup another day.

10. Rinse the inside and outside of the chicken with running cold water. Drain the chicken and pat it dry with paper towels. Discard the towels.

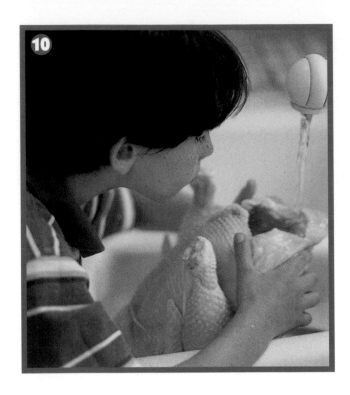

▲ **13.** Place the roasting pan in the oven on the middle rack. Turn the oven control to 350° F. Set the timer and roast the chicken and vegetables for 2 hours.

When the timer goes off, begin testing the chicken for doneness. It is fully roasted when the temperature on the *meat thermometer* or *the instant-read thermometer* registers 175° to 180° F or the juices run clear when the thickest part of the thigh is pierced with the *paring knife* or *fork* (see pages 19–20 for complete instructions).

When the chicken is fully roasted, turn off the oven. Using the pot holders, place the roasting pan on the trivet.

Place the chicken on the rack in the roasting pan. Rub the chicken all over with the cut sides of the lemon while gently squeezing the lemon to release some juice. Place the lemon halves inside the chicken.

11. Using your fingers, rub the chicken with the thyme mixture. *Wash your hands and all work surfaces that have come in contact with raw chicken before going on to any other food preparation.*

12. If you have a *meat thermometer,* insert it into the thickest part of the chicken thigh, next to the body. Be very careful that the pointed end of the thermometer does not touch the thighbone.

If you have an *instant-read thermometer,* do *not* insert it into the chicken until you are ready to test for doneness.

14. Tear off a piece of aluminum foil. Place the foil over the chicken and vegetables.

Set the timer and let the chicken and vegetables stand for 5 minutes. This will make cutting the chicken easier.

his is so full of savory vegetables, no one will ever miss the meat!

Vegetable Chili

25 minutes
PREPARATION

1 hour
COOKING

1 hour 25 minutes
TOTAL TIME

DEGREE OF DIFFICULTY: **MODERATE**
SERVINGS: **8**

UTENSILS

Cutting board
Measuring spoons
1-cup dry measuring cup
Paring knife
3 small mixing bowls
Vegetable brush
Strainer
Can opener
Medium-size mixing bowl
5-quart saucepot with lid
Timer
Pot holder
Wooden spoon
3-quart saucepan with lid
Ladle
Serving bowls

INGREDIENTS

2 large garlic cloves
1 large green pepper (about 8 ounces)
2 medium-size zucchini (8 ounces each)
1 large onion (about 8 ounces)

1 can black beans (15- to 19-ounce size)
1 can red kidney beans (15- to 19-ounce size)
1 can vegetable broth (14½-ounce size) or beef broth (13¾- to 14½-ounce size)
1 can whole tomatoes (28-ounce size)
2 tablespoons vegetable oil
1 tablespoon plus 1½ teaspoons chili powder
1 teaspoon dried oregano leaves
1 can corn kernels (8¾-ounce size)
2 cups regular long-grain rice
2 cups shredded Monterey Jack or Cheddar cheese or reduced fat Monterey Jack or Cheddar cheese (8 ounces)

▲**1.** Place the garlic cloves on the cutting board. With the paring knife, cut off the stem ends of each one. With the paring knife or your fingers, peel off the skins. Discard the ends and skins. With the paring knife, chop the garlic cloves. Put the pieces in one of the small mixing bowls.

2. Rinse the pepper with running cold water. With the vegetable brush, scrub the zucchini while rinsing them under running cold water. Pat the vegetables dry. Set the zucchini aside.

▲**3.** Place the pepper on the cutting board. With the paring knife, cut it lengthwise in half. With the paring knife or your fingers, remove and discard the seeds and white ribs.

With the paring knife, cut each half lengthwise into 1-inch strips. Then cut the strips crosswise into 1-inch pieces. Set the pieces aside.

▲**4.** Place the zucchini on the cutting board. With the paring knife, cut off and discard the ends. With the paring knife, cut each zucchini lengthwise in half. Place each half, flat side down, on the cutting board. Cut each half crosswise into 1-inch pieces. Put the pieces in the second small mixing bowl.

▲**5.** Place the onion on the cutting board. With the paring knife, cut off the ends. With the paring knife or your fingers, peel off the skin. Discard the ends and skin.

With the paring knife, cut the onion lengthwise in half. Place each half, flat side down, on the cutting board. Cut each half lengthwise into ½-inch strips. Then cut the strips crosswise into ½-inch pieces. Put the pieces in the mixing bowl with the garlic.

Since onions usually make the eyes tear, be careful not to put your face too close to the onion. Do not wipe your eyes with your hands if they have onion juice on them. Wash your hands before continuing with the recipe.

6. Place the strainer in the sink. Using the can opener, open both cans of beans. Pour the beans into the strainer and rinse them with running cold water. Once they have drained, set the beans aside in the third small mixing bowl.

7. Using the can opener, open the cans of broth and tomatoes. Pour the tomatoes with their liquid into the medium-size mixing bowl. Using your fingers, break up the tomatoes into small pieces. Set them aside.

▲**8.** Heat the vegetable oil in the saucepot on the stove over a medium heat. Add the garlic mixture. Set the timer and cook it for 5 minutes. Holding the handle of the saucepot with the pot holder, stir the garlic occasionally with the wooden spoon.

▲**9.** Add the pepper, chili powder, and oregano. Set the timer and cook the mixture for 5 minutes. Holding the handle of the saucepot with the pot holder, stir the mixture occasionally with the wooden spoon.

▲**10.** Add the tomatoes with their liquid and the broth. Holding the handle of the saucepot with the pot holder, stir the mixture with the wooden spoon.

▲**11.** Bring the mixture to a boil over a high heat. Turn down the heat to low. Cover the saucepot with the lid. Set the timer and simmer the mixture for 15 minutes.

12. Wash the strainer and place it in the sink. Using the can opener, open the can of corn kernels. Pour them into the strainer to drain off the liquid.

▲ **13.** Add the zucchini, beans, and corn to the saucepot. Holding the handle of the saucepot with the pot holder, stir the mixture with the wooden spoon.

▲ **14.** Bring the mixture to a boil over a high heat. Turn down the heat to low. Cover the saucepot with the lid.

Set the timer and simmer the chili mixture for 30 minutes.

▲ **15.** While the chili is simmering, prepare the rice as the package instructions direct, using the saucepan.

To serve, spoon some rice into each serving bowl. Holding the handle of the saucepot with the pot holder, use the ladle to pour some Vegetable Chili over the rice. Sprinkle each serving with some cheese.

SHORTCUT VEGETABLE CHILI

15 minutes   1 hour 5 minutes
PREPARATION   COOKING

1 hour 20 minutes
TOTAL TIME

DEGREE OF DIFFICULTY: **EASY**
SERVINGS: **8**

INGREDIENTS
2 large garlic cloves
1 can black beans (15- to 19-ounce size)
1 can red kidney beans (15- to 19-ounce size)
1 can vegetable broth (14½-ounce size) or beef broth (13¾- to 14½-ounce size)
1 can whole tomatoes (28-ounce size)
2 tablespoons vegetable oil
1 cup frozen chopped onion
2 cups frozen cut sweet peppers (red and green)
1 tablespoon plus 1½ teaspoons chili powder
1 teaspoon dried oregano leaves
1 cup frozen corn kernels
2 cups frozen cut zucchini
2 cups regular long-grain rice
2 cups shredded Monterey Jack or Cheddar cheese or reduced fat Monterey Jack or Cheddar cheese (8 ounces)

▲ **1.** Follow step 1 in the Vegetable Chili recipe.

2. Omit steps 2, 3, 4, and 5.

▲ **3.** Follow steps 6, 7, and 8, but use the frozen onion instead of the fresh one.

▲ **4.** Follow steps 9, 10, 11, and 13, but use the frozen vegetables instead of the fresh ones.

▲ **5.** Follow steps 14 and 15.

This flavorful mixture is packed into muffin cups to shorten the cooking time. You can double the recipe and use the leftovers as sandwich fillings.

Mini Meat Loaves

25 minutes
PREPARATION

40 minutes
COOKING

1 hour 5 minutes
TOTAL TIME

DEGREE OF DIFFICULTY: **MODERATE**
SERVINGS: **6**

UTENSILS
Cutting board
1-cup liquid measuring cup
½-cup dry measuring cup
Measuring spoons
Muffin pan with six 2½-by-1¼-inch cups
Paring knife
Grater
Large mixing bowl
Strainer
Can opener
Small bowl or cup
Pot holders
15½-inch-by-10½-inch jelly-roll pan or
    aluminum foil
Timer
Trivet
Instant-read thermometer or
    2 forks and plate

INGREDIENTS
Nonstick cooking spray
1 small onion (about 3 ounces)
1 can whole corn kernels (8¾-ounce size) or
    1 cup frozen corn kernels, thawed
1 large egg
¾ pound lean ground beef
½ pound ground turkey
½ cup chili sauce
½ cup plain dried bread crumbs
1½ teaspoons chili powder
½ teaspoon salt
¼ teaspoon pepper

▲ **1.** Preheat the oven to 350° F.

2. Spray the muffin cups with the nonstick cooking spray; set the muffin pan aside.

▲3. Place the onion on the cutting board. With the paring knife, cut off the ends. With the paring knife or your fingers, peel off the skin. Discard the ends and skin.

Place the grater in the mixing bowl. Rub the onion along the side of the grater with the medium-size holes. *Do this slowly and carefully so that you do not scrape your knuckles. Stop when the onion gets too small.*

Since onions usually make the eyes tear, be careful not to put your face too close to the onion. Do not wipe your eyes with your hands if they have onion juice on them. Wash your hands before continuing with the recipe.

4. If you are using *canned corn,* place the strainer in the sink. Using the can opener, open the can of corn kernels. Pour the kernels into the strainer to drain off the liquid. Put the kernels in the mixing bowl.

If you are using *frozen corn,* put the thawed kernels in the mixing bowl.

5. Crack the egg into a small bowl; discard the shells.

Put the cracked egg, ground beef, ground turkey, chili sauce, bread crumbs, chili powder, salt, and pepper in the mixing bowl.

6. Using your hands, mix the ground meat mixture until it is well combined. Then divide it into 6 even portions.

Wet your hands with cold water, and shape each portion of ground meat mixture into a large meatball. Place each meatball in a greased muffin cup. *Wash your hands and all work surfaces that have come in contact with raw ground meat before going on to any other food preparation.*

If you have an *instant-read thermometer,* do not insert it into a meatball until you are ready to test for doneness.

▲7. Using the pot holders, place the muffin pan in the oven. Place the jelly-roll pan or a piece of aluminum foil on the rack below to catch any drips. Set the timer and bake the meat loaves for 40 minutes.

When the timer goes off, begin testing the meat loaves for doneness. They are fully baked when the temperature on the *instant-read thermometer* registers at least 165° F or when they have lost their pink color throughout when cut with the *paring knife* (see pages 18–19 for complete instructions). When they are fully baked, turn off the oven.

Serve the Mini Meat Loaves right away.

HINT: This recipe can be made entirely with lean ground beef. Just increase the amount of ground beef to 1¼ pounds.

Here is a quick and tasty dinner idea. Apples add a natural sweetness to the pork.

Glazed Pork Chops with Apples

20 minutes
PREPARATION

20 minutes
COOKING

40 minutes
TOTAL TIME

DEGREE OF DIFFICULTY: **MODERATE**
SERVINGS: **4**

UTENSILS
Cutting board
Measuring spoons
1-cup liquid measuring cup
12-inch piece waxed paper
Spoon
Vegetable peeler
Paring knife
Melon baller
Fork
2 plates
12-inch nonstick skillet
Pot holder
Tongs
Timer
Trivet
Serving platter
Aluminum foil
Wooden spoon

INGREDIENTS
3 tablespoons all-purpose flour
½ teaspoon salt
⅛ teaspoon pepper
2 medium-size red cooking apples,
    such as McIntosh or Rome Beauty
    (about 1 pound)
4 pork loin chops, each ½ inch thick
    (about 1½ pounds)
3 teaspoons vegetable oil
¾ cup apple juice
½ cup chicken broth
1 teaspoon Dijon mustard

1. Put the flour, salt, and pepper on the waxed paper. With the spoon, stir the mixture until it is well combined. Set the flour mixture aside.

▲**2.** Place the apples on the cutting board. Using the vegetable peeler, peel off and discard the skins.

   With the paring knife, cut each apple in half lengthwise, starting at the stem end.

With the melon baller, scoop out and discard the seeds and core.

Place each half, flat side down, on the cutting board. With the paring knife, cut each half lengthwise into 6 pieces. Set the pieces aside.

3. Holding each pork chop with the fork or your fingers, dip both sides of it into the flour mixture to coat well. Place the coated chops on one of the plates.

▲**4.** Heat the vegetable oil in the skillet on the stove over a medium heat.

Holding the handle of the skillet with the pot holder, use the tongs to place the pork chops gently in the skillet.

Set the timer and cook the pork chops for 5 minutes, or until they are browned. To see if they are browned, hold the handle of the skillet with the pot holder, lift up one end of each chop with the washed tongs, and take a look. If they are not browned, set the timer and cook for 1 to 2 minutes more.

▲**5.** Holding the handle of the skillet with the pot holder, turn the pork chops over with the tongs. Set the timer and cook the pork chops for 3 to 5 minutes, or until this side is browned.

When the pork chops are browned, begin testing them for doneness by cutting into them with the paring knife to see if they have lost their pink color throughout (see page 18 for complete instructions). When the chops are fully cooked, using the tongs, put them on the serving platter. Cover the platter with aluminum foil to keep the pork chops warm.

▲**6.** Put the skillet back on the stove. Add the apple pieces. Set the timer and cook the apples for 3 minutes over a medium heat. Holding the handle of the skillet with the pot holder, stir the apples occasionally with the wooden spoon.

▲**7.** Add the apple juice, broth, and Dijon mustard. Holding the handle of the skillet with the pot holder, stir the mixture and scrape up any brown bits from the bottom of the skillet with the wooden spoon.

Bring the mixture to a boil over a high heat. Set the timer and boil the mixture for 2 to 4 minutes. Turn off the heat.

▲**8.** Holding the handle of the skillet with the pot holder, place the skillet on the trivet. Remove the aluminum foil from the serving platter and discard. Spoon the apple mixture over the pork chops.

Simple to make, this basic tomato sauce can easily be varied by adding different ingredients.

Tomato Sauce

BASIC TOMATO SAUCE

20 minutes	40 minutes	1 hour
PREPARATION	COOKING	TOTAL TIME

DEGREE OF DIFFICULTY: **MODERATE**
SERVINGS: **6**

UTENSILS

Cutting board
¼-cup dry measuring cup
Measuring spoons
Paring knife
Can opener
Medium-size mixing bowl
5-quart saucepot
Timer
Pot holder
Wooden spoon

INGREDIENTS

2 large garlic cloves
1 medium-size onion (about 4 ounces)
2 cans Italian plum tomatoes (28-ounce
    size)
¼ cup packed fresh basil leaves or
    1 teaspoon dried basil leaves
2 tablespoons olive oil
½ teaspoon salt
¼ teaspoon pepper

▲**1.** Place the garlic cloves on the cutting board. With the paring knife, cut off the stem ends. With the paring knife or your fingers, peel off the skins. Discard the ends and skins.

Cut each clove lengthwise into thin slices. Set the slices aside.

▲**2.** Place the onion on the cutting board. With the paring knife, cut off the ends. With the paring knife or your fingers, peel off the skin. Discard the ends and skin.

With the paring knife, dice the onion. Set the pieces aside. *Since onions usually make the eyes tear, be careful not to put your face too close to the onion. Do not wipe your eyes with your hands if they have onion juice on them. Wash your hands before continuing.*

3. Using the can opener, open the cans of tomatoes. Pour the tomatoes with their liquid into the mixing bowl. Using your fingers, break up the tomatoes into small pieces. Set them aside.

▲**4.** If you are using *fresh basil leaves,* place the leaves one on top of the other on the cutting board. With the paring knife, chop them. Set the pieces aside.

▲**5.** Heat the olive oil in the saucepot on the stove over a medium heat. Add the garlic and onion. Set the timer and cook the mixture for 5 minutes. Holding the handle of the saucepot with the pot holder, stir the mixture occasionally with the wooden spoon.

▲**6.** Add the tomatoes with their liquid, salt, pepper, and the dried basil, if you are using this instead of fresh basil. Holding the handle of the saucepot with the pot holder, stir the mixture with the wooden spoon.

▲**7.** Bring the mixture to a boil over a high heat. Then turn down the heat to low. Set the timer and simmer the mixture for 30 minutes. Holding the handle of the saucepot with the pot holder, stir the mixture occasionally with the wooden spoon.

▲**8.** Add the *fresh basil* if you are using this instead of the dried basil. Set the timer and cook the sauce for 5 minutes. Turn off the heat.

Put any extra tomato sauce in a food storage container. It will keep for up to 5 days in the refrigerator or 3 months in the freezer.

TOMATO SAUCE WITH MUSHROOMS

15 minutes
PREPARATION

40 minutes
COOKING

55 minutes
TOTAL TIME

ADDITIONAL INGREDIENTS
20 medium-size mushrooms
   (about ½ pound)
½ teaspoon dried thyme leaves (instead
   of fresh or dried basil leaves)

▲**1.** Rinse the mushrooms with running cold water. Pat them dry.

Place the mushrooms on the cutting board. With the paring knife, cut off and discard the end of each stem.

Cut each mushroom lengthwise into thin slices. Set the slices aside.

▲**2.** Follow steps 1, 2, 3, and 5 in the Basic Tomato Sauce recipe.

▲**3.** Add the mushrooms to the mixture in the saucepot. Set the timer and cook the mixture for 5 minutes. Holding the handle of the saucepot with the pot holder, stir the mixture occasionally with the wooden spoon.

▲**4.** Follow steps 6 and 7, but use the dried thyme instead of the basil leaves.

▲**5.** Turn off the heat.

This yummy recipe is sure to be everyone's favorite dinner.

Spaghetti and Meatballs

 25 minutes
PREPARATION

 50 minutes
COOKING

 1 hour 15 minutes
TOTAL TIME

DEGREE OF DIFFICULTY: **MODERATE**

SERVINGS: **6**

UTENSILS
Cutting board
Measuring spoons
Paring knife
2 medium-size mixing bowls
Small bowl or cup
2 plates
5-quart saucepot
Wooden spoon
Timer
Pot holders
Spoon
Can opener
6-quart saucepot
Slotted spoon
Fork
Colander
Trivet
Serving bowls
Ladle

INGREDIENTS

Meatballs

1 large garlic clove
About 10 sprigs flat-leaf Italian parsley
1 large egg
½ pound lean ground beef
3 tablespoons plain dried bread crumbs
3 tablespoons grated Parmesan cheese
¼ teaspoon salt
¼ teaspoon pepper
1 tablespoon olive oil

Tomato Sauce

2 large garlic cloves
2 cans Italian plum tomatoes (28-ounce
   size)
1 tablespoon olive oil
½ teaspoon salt
½ teaspoon pepper

Spaghetti

1 package spaghetti or other macaroni,
   such as linguine, penne, rotelle, or
   radiatore (16-ounce size)

SERVING SUGGESTION
Grated Parmesan cheese

▲ **1.** *To make the meatballs,* place the garlic clove on the cutting board. With the paring knife, cut off the stem end. With the paring knife or your fingers, peel off the skin. Discard the end and skin. With the paring knife, chop the garlic clove. Put the pieces in one of the mixing bowls.

▲ **2.** Rinse the parsley with running cold water. Pat it dry.

Place the parsley on the cutting board. Using your fingers, pull off the parsley leaves from the stems. Discard the stems.

With the paring knife, chop enough parsley to measure 2 tablespoons. Put the pieces in the mixing bowl with the garlic.

3. Crack the egg into the small bowl; discard the shells.

Put the cracked egg, ground beef, bread crumbs, Parmesan cheese, salt, and pepper in the mixing bowl. Using your hands, mix the ground beef mixture until it is well combined.

4. Using your hands, divide the ground beef mixture into 12 even portions. Place each portion on one of the plates.

Wet your hands with cold water and shape each portion of ground beef mixture into a meatball. Place each one back on the plate. *Wash your hands and all work surfaces that have come in contact with raw ground meat before going on to any other food preparation.*

▲**5.** Heat the olive oil in the 5-quart saucepot on the stove over a medium heat. Using the wooden spoon, put the meatballs in the saucepot. Set the timer and cook the meatballs for 10 minutes. Holding the handle of the saucepot with a pot holder, use the spoon to turn them occasionally so that they become brown on all sides.

When the meatballs have browned, hold the handle of the saucepot with a pot holder and use the spoon to put the meatballs on the other plate.

▲**6.** While the meatballs are browning, prepare the tomato sauce.

To prepare the tomato sauce, place the garlic cloves on the cutting board. With the paring knife, cut off the stem ends. With the paring knife or your fingers, peel off the skins. Discard the ends and skins. With the paring knife, cut each garlic clove lengthwise into thin slices. Set them aside.

7. Using the can opener, open the cans of tomatoes. Pour the tomatoes with their liquid into the other mixing bowl. Using your fingers, break up the tomatoes into small pieces.

▲**8.** Pour the olive oil into the saucepot in which the meatballs were browned. Heat the olive oil on the stove over a medium heat. Add the garlic. Set the timer and cook the garlic for 2 minutes. Holding the handle of the saucepot with a pot holder, stir the garlic occasionally with the washed wooden spoon.

▲**9.** Add the plum tomatoes with their liquid and the salt and pepper. Holding the handle of the saucepot with a pot holder, stir the mixture with the wooden spoon.

Bring the mixture to a boil over a high heat. Turn down the heat to low. Set the timer and simmer the mixture for 20 minutes. Holding the handle of the saucepot with a pot holder, stir the mixture occasionally with the wooden spoon.

▲**10.** Holding the handle of the saucepot with a pot holder, use the spoon to put the meatballs back into the saucepot. Bring the mixture to a boil over a high heat. Turn down the heat to low. Set the timer and simmer the mixture for 15 minutes.

▲**11.** While the sauce is coming to a boil, prepare the spaghetti as the package instructions direct, using the 6-quart saucepot.

When it is time to test the spaghetti for doneness, rinse a piece under running cold water to cool it well and then taste it to see if it is al dente (see page 21 for complete instructions).

When the spaghetti is fully cooked, turn off the heat. Place the colander in the sink. Have an adult pour the cooked spaghetti into the colander to drain the water well. *Boiling water is dangerous. Do not pour the cooked spaghetti into the colander yourself.*

▲**12.** When the timer for the tomato sauce goes off, turn off the heat. Holding the handle of the saucepot with a pot holder, place the saucepot on the trivet. To serve, spoon some spaghetti into each serving bowl. Holding the handle of the saucepot with a pot holder, use the ladle to pour some tomato sauce and meatballs over the spaghetti.

This is a light yet hearty pasta sauce that gets lots of flavor from the turkey sausage.

Pasta with Sausage and Vegetables

20 minutes
PREPARATION

25 minutes
COOKING

45 minutes
TOTAL TIME

DEGREE OF DIFFICULTY: **MODERATE**
SERVINGS: **4**

UTENSILS
Cutting board
Measuring spoons
1-cup liquid measuring cup
Paring knife
1-cup dry measuring cup
3 small mixing bowls
Can opener
Kitchen shears
12-inch skillet with lid
Timer
Pot holders

Wooden spoon
Slotted spoon
5-quart saucepot
Fork
Colander
Ladle
Serving bowls

INGREDIENTS

1 bunch broccoli (about 1 pound)
1 large red or green pepper (about 8 ounces)
1 can whole tomatoes (14½- to 16-ounce size)
¾ pound sweet or hot Italian turkey sausage
2 tablespoons olive oil
½ cup chicken broth
½ package rotelle or radiatore macaroni
      (16-ounce size)

SERVING SUGGESTION

Grated Parmesan cheese

1. Rinse the broccoli and pepper with running cold water. Pat them dry. Set the pepper aside.

▲**2.** Place the broccoli on the cutting board. With the paring knife, cut off enough flowerets to measure 3 cups. If any are large, cut them lengthwise in half. Put the flowerets in one of the mixing bowls and set them aside.

▲**3.** Place the pepper on the cutting board. With the paring knife, cut it lengthwise in half. With the paring knife or your fingers, remove and discard the seeds and white ribs.

   With the paring knife, cut each half lengthwise into thin strips. Set them aside.

4. Using the can opener, open the can of tomatoes. Pour the tomatoes with their liquid into the second mixing bowl. Using your fingers, break up the tomatoes into small pieces. Set them aside.

▲**5.** Put the sausage on the cutting board. Using the kitchen shears or the paring knife, cut away and discard the sausage casings. Using your fingers, break up the sausage into small pieces.

▲**6.** Heat 1 tablespoon of olive oil in the skillet on the stove over a medium heat. Add the sausage.

   Set the timer and cook the sausage for 5 minutes, or until it is browned and loses its pink color throughout. Holding the handle of the skillet with a pot holder, stir the sausage frequently with the wooden spoon.

▲**7.** Holding the handle of the skillet with a pot holder, use the slotted spoon to put the sausage in the third mixing bowl. Set the sausage aside.

▲**8.** Heat 1 tablespoon of olive oil in the skillet on the stove over a medium heat.

▲**9.** Add the pepper pieces.

▲**10.** Set the timer and cook the pepper for 2 minutes. Holding the handle of the skillet with a pot holder, stir the pepper occasionally with the wooden spoon.

▲**11.** Add the broccoli flowerets, tomatoes with their liquid, turkey sausage, and chicken broth. Holding the handle of the skillet with a pot holder, stir the mixture and scrape up any brown bits from the bottom of the skillet with the wooden spoon.

▲**12.** Bring the mixture to a boil over a high heat. Set the timer and boil the mixture for 5 minutes. Turn down the heat to low. Cover the skillet with the lid. Set the timer and simmer the mixture for 5 minutes.

▲**13.** While the pasta sauce is coming to a boil, prepare the macaroni as the package instructions direct, using the saucepot.

When it is time to test the macaroni for doneness, rinse a piece under running cold water to cool it well and then taste it to see if it is al dente (see page 21 for complete instructions).

When the macaroni is fully cooked, turn off the heat. Place the colander in the sink. Have an adult pour the cooked macaroni into the colander to drain the water well. *Boiling water is dangerous. Do not pour the cooked macaroni into the colander yourself.*

▲**14.** When the timer for the pasta sauce goes off, turn off the heat.

To serve, spoon some macaroni into each serving bowl. Holding the handle of the skillet with the pot holder, use the ladle to pour some sausage and vegetables over the macaroni. Sprinkle each serving with grated Parmesan cheese.

PASTA WITH SAUSAGE AND FROZEN VEGETABLES

10 minutes	25 minutes	35 minutes
PREPARATION	COOKING	TOTAL TIME

DEGREE OF DIFFICULTY: **EASY**

SERVINGS: **4**

INGREDIENTS

1 can whole tomatoes (14½- to 16-ounce size)
¾ pound sweet or hot Italian turkey sausage
2 tablespoons olive oil
1 package frozen broccoli, cauliflower, and
    red pepper combination (16-ounce size)
½ cup chicken broth
½ package rotelle or radiatore macaroni
    (16-ounce size)

SERVING SUGGESTION

Grated Parmesan cheese

1. Omit steps 1, 2, and 3 in the Pasta with Sausage and Vegetables recipe.

▲**2.** Follow steps 4, 5, 6, 7, and 8.

▲**3.** Follow step 9, but use the package of frozen vegetables instead of the pepper.

▲**4.** Set the timer and cook the vegetables for 5 minutes. Holding the handle of the skillet with a pot holder, stir the vegetables occasionally with the wooden spoon.

▲**5.** Add the tomatoes with their liquid, turkey sausage, and chicken broth to the skillet. Holding the handle of the skillet with a pot holder, stir the mixture and scrape up any brown bits from the bottom of the skillet with the wooden spoon.

▲**6.** Follow step 12, but set the timer and simmer the mixture for 8 minutes.

▲**7.** Follow steps 13 and 14.

Snacks, Salads, and Side Dishes

◆ ◆ ◆ ◆ ◆ ◆ ◆ ◆ ◆ ◆ ◆ ◆ ◆ ◆ ◆ ◆ ◆ ◆

Here's a fun and easy snack to prepare when friends come over after school.

Peanutty Popcorn

10 minutes
PREPARATION

5 minutes
COOKING

15 minutes
TOTAL TIME

DEGREE OF DIFFICULTY: **EASY**

SERVINGS: **4 TO 6**

UTENSILS
Cutting board
1-cup and ½-cup dry measuring cups
1-cup liquid measuring cup
Large mixing bowl
Rubber spatula
1-quart saucepan
Timer
Pot holder
Wooden spoon

INGREDIENTS
8 cups popped corn or ½ cup unpopped
   corn kernels
⅔ cup light corn syrup
½ cup smooth peanut butter
1 cup dark seedless raisins
½ cup shelled raw sunflower seeds

1. If you are using *popped corn,* put it in the mixing bowl. If you are using *unpopped kernels,* prepare them according to the package instructions. Then put the popped corn in the mixing bowl. Set the popcorn aside.

▲**2.** Using the spatula, scrape the corn syrup and peanut butter into the saucepan. Set the timer and cook the mixture on the stove over a medium heat for 5 minutes, or until it is well combined. Holding the handle of the saucepan with the pot holder, stir the mixture occasionally with the wooden spoon.

▲**3.** Turn off the heat. Holding the handle of the saucepan with the pot holder, pour the mixture over the popped corn.

4. Stir the popped corn and the peanut butter mixture with the wooden spoon. Add the raisins and sunflower seeds. Stir the ingredients until everything is well combined and evenly coated.

This is a cool and creamy after-school treat. It can be served with homemade tortilla chips, which are healthier than store-bought ones.

Guacamole

25 minutes
PREPARATION

10 minutes
COOKING

35 minutes
TOTAL TIME

DEGREE OF DIFFICULTY: **EASY**

SERVINGS: **4**

UTENSILS
Cutting board
Measuring spoons
Paring knife
Spoon
Mixing bowl
Fork or potato masher
Small bowl or cup
Pastry brush
15½-inch-by-10½-inch jelly-roll pan
Pot holders
Timer
Wire rack
Basket or bowl

INGREDIENTS

Guacamole

2 plum tomatoes (4 ounces)

1 scallion

1 avocado (about 10 ounces)

3 tablespoons sour cream or light
   or fat free sour cream

2 teaspoons lemon juice

⅛ teaspoon salt

Hot pepper sauce (optional)

Tortilla Chips

¼ teaspoon chili powder

⅛ teaspoon salt

4 corn tortillas (about 6 inches in diameter)

1 teaspoon vegetable oil

▲**1.** Preheat the oven to 400° F.

▲**2.** *To prepare the Guacamole,* rinse the tomatoes and scallion with running cold water. Pat them dry. Set the scallion aside.

Place the tomatoes on the cutting board. With the paring knife, remove and discard the core from each tomato. Cut each tomato lengthwise in half, starting at the stem end.

Dice the tomatoes. Set the pieces aside.

▲**3.** Place the scallion on the cutting board. With the paring knife, cut off the roots and trim off the dark green ends. Discard the roots and ends.

Cut the scallion crosswise into thin slices. Set the slices aside.

▲**4.** Place the avocado on the cutting board. With the paring knife, cut it lengthwise in

half, starting at the stem end. Cut around the large pit in the center.

Holding the avocado with your hands, gently twist the halves to separate them.

Using the spoon, scoop out the pit from the avocado half. Scoop out the flesh from the skin and put it in the mixing bowl. Discard the pit and skin.

5. Using the fork, mash the avocado until it is almost smooth.

6. Add the tomatoes, scallion, sour cream, lemon juice, and salt. Using the spoon, stir the mixture until it is well combined.

7. If you like your food a little spicy or hot, add some hot pepper sauce, one shake at a time, to the Guacamole. Stir the Guacamole with the spoon and taste it after each addition of hot pepper sauce.

HOW TO CHOOSE AND RIPEN AN AVOCADO

An avocado is a fruit known for its rich, buttery texture. Depending upon the variety, it can be green with a thin, smooth skin or purplish black with a pebbly skin. A ripe avocado should be firm yet should yield slightly if you squeeze it lightly. To ripen an avocado, place it in a paper bag for 2 to 4 days at room temperature. Store ripe avocados in the refrigerator and use them within 3 to 5 days.

8. *To prepare the Tortilla Chips,* put the chili powder and salt in the small bowl. Using a measuring spoon, stir the mixture until it is well combined. Set the chili powder mixture aside.

9. Place the tortillas on the cutting board. Dip the pastry brush into the small bowl containing the vegetable oil. Brush one side of each tortilla with the oil. Sprinkle each one with some chili powder mixture.

▲ **10.** Stack the tortillas one on top of another. With the paring knife, cut them into 8 pieces. Arrange the pieces in a single layer in the jelly-roll pan.

▲ **11.** Using the pot holders, place the pan in the oven. Set the timer and bake the pieces for 8 minutes, or until they are crisp and lightly browned.

▲ **12.** Using the pot holders, remove the pan from the oven. Place it on the wire rack. Turn off the oven. Set the timer and let the pieces cool for 5 minutes.

13. Put the Tortilla Chips in a basket or bowl and serve with the Guacamole.

If you are not serving the Guacamole right away, press a piece of plastic wrap directly onto it and refrigerate. This will keep the Guacamole from discoloring.

Everyone can join in the fun of making these fancy fruit treats.

Fruit Kabobs

15 minutes
PREPARATION

0 minutes
COOKING

15 minutes
TOTAL TIME

DEGREE OF DIFFICULTY: **EASY**
SERVINGS: **4**

UTENSILS

Cutting board
½-cup and ¼-cup dry measuring cups
1-cup liquid measuring cup
Measuring spoons
Rubber spatula
Small mixing bowl
Spoon
Paring knife
Melon baller
Long skewers or wooden picks
Serving platter
Small bowls

INGREDIENTS

Peanut Butter Dipping Sauce

½ cup smooth peanut butter
¼ cup plain low fat yogurt
¼ cup water
2 tablespoons flaked coconut
2 tablespoons honey

Fruit Kabobs

1 medium-size red or green apple (about 5 ounces)
1 medium-size red or green pear (about 7 ounces)
2 medium-size bananas (about 12 ounces)

1. *To prepare the Peanut Butter Dipping Sauce,* use the spatula to scrape the peanut butter and yogurt into the mixing bowl. Add the water, coconut, and honey. With the spoon, stir the mixture until it is well combined. Set the Peanut Butter Dipping Sauce aside.

2. *To prepare the Fruit Kabobs,* rinse the apple and pear with running cold water. Pat them dry.

▲ **3.** Place the apple and pear on the cutting board. With the paring knife, cut the apple lengthwise in half, starting at the stem end.

With the melon baller, scoop out and discard the seeds and core.

Place each half, flat side down, on the cutting board. With the paring knife, cut each half lengthwise into 4 pieces. Cut each piece crosswise into 3 pieces. Set the pieces aside.

▲ **4.** With the paring knife, cut the pear lengthwise in half, starting at the stem end.

With the melon baller, scoop out and discard the seeds and core.

Place each half, flat side down, on the cutting board. With the paring knife, cut each half lengthwise into 4 pieces. Cut each piece crosswise into 3 pieces. Set the pieces aside.

▲ **5.** Place the bananas on the cutting board. Peel off and discard the skins.

With the paring knife, cut each banana crosswise into 6 equal pieces. Set the pieces aside.

▲ **6.** Push some pieces of each type of fruit onto a skewer, starting from the pointed end.

Repeat this step until all the fruit is arranged on the skewers.

Place the Fruit Kabobs on a serving platter. Spoon some Peanut Butter Dipping Sauce into each of the small bowls and serve.

Keep this cool and refreshing salad handy in your refrigerator for a snack any time of day.

Fruit Salad

20 minutes
PREPARATION

5 minutes
COOKING

25 minutes
TOTAL TIME

DEGREE OF DIFFICULTY: **EASY**

SERVINGS: **4**

UTENSILS
Cutting board
¼-cup and 1-cup dry measuring cups
Measuring spoons
Paring knife
Melon baller
Medium-size mixing bowl
Rubber spatula
1-quart saucepan
Timer
Pot holder
Wooden spoon
Trivet

INGREDIENTS

Assorted seasonal fruits, such as apples,
    apricots, bananas, blueberries,
    cherries, seedless grapes, melon,
    oranges, peaches, pears, pineapple,
    plums, raspberries, strawberries
¼ cup apple jelly
1 tablespoon chopped fresh mint leaves or
    1 teaspoon dried mint leaves

▲ **1.** Wash the fruits you have chosen with running cold water and pat them dry. Place them on the cutting board.

If you are using *apples, apricots, cherries, peaches, pears, or plums,* cut the fruits in half with the paring knife. Remove the seeds and cores with the melon baller and discard. Remove the pits with your fingers and discard.

If you are using *bananas, melons, oranges, or pineapple,* remove and discard the peels or rinds.

If you are using *strawberries,* remove and discard the stems. If you are using *blueberries,* pick out and discard any stems and any shriveled berries. If you are using *raspberries,* pick out and discard soft or moldy-looking berries.

▲ **2.** With the paring knife, cut the fruits into 1-inch pieces. Cut enough to measure 5 cups. Put the pieces in the mixing bowl. Set the fruits aside.

▲ **3.** Using the spatula, scrape the apple jelly into the saucepan. Set the timer and cook the jelly on the stove over a low heat for 5 minutes. Holding the handle of the saucepan with the pot holder, stir the jelly occasionally with the wooden spoon. When it melts and is smooth, turn off the heat.

▲ **4.** Holding the handle of the saucepan with the pot holder, remove the saucepan from the stove and place it on the trivet. Set the timer and let the apple jelly cool for 3 minutes.

▲ **5.** Holding the handle of the saucepan with the pot holder, use the spatula to scrape the apple jelly into the mixing bowl. Add the mint. Using the spatula, gently stir the Fruit Salad until it is well combined.

The Fruit Salad will keep in the refrigerator for two days. If you used bananas, raspberries, or strawberries, keep it just one day because these fruits tend to get soft.

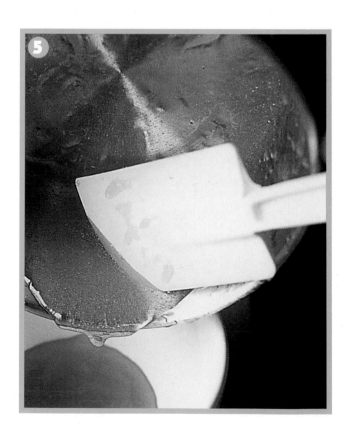

You'll love leftover chicken once you've tasted it in this delicious crunchy guise.

Chicken and Apple Salad

25 minutes
PREPARATION

0 minutes
COOKING

25 minutes
TOTAL TIME

DEGREE OF DIFFICULTY: **EASY**

SERVINGS: **4**

UTENSILS
Cutting board
⅓-cup, 1-cup, and ¼-cup dry
     measuring cups
Measuring spoons
Rubber spatula
Medium-size mixing bowl
Spoon
Paring knife
Vegetable peeler
Melon baller

INGREDIENTS
⅓ cup plain low fat yogurt
⅓ cup mayonnaise or reduced fat
     or fat free mayonnaise
1 tablespoon plus 1 teaspoon prepared
     or Dijon mustard
1 teaspoon lemon juice
¼ teaspoon salt
⅛ teaspoon pepper
2 large celery stalks (about 4 ounces)

1 large carrot (3 ounces)
1 red apple, such as McIntosh or
     Red Delicious (6 ounces)
2 slices Jarlsberg cheese or Swiss cheese
2 cups cooked chicken or turkey, cut into
     1-inch pieces (about 10 ounces)
¼ cup walnut pieces

SERVING SUGGESTION
Bagel chips

1. Using the spatula, scrape the yogurt and mayonnaise into the mixing bowl. Add the mustard, lemon juice, salt, and pepper. With the spoon, stir the mixture until it is well combined. Set the yogurt dressing aside.

2. Rinse the celery and apple with running cold water. Pat them dry. Set the apple aside.

▲**3.** Place the celery on the cutting board. With the paring knife, cut off and discard the ends.

Dice each celery stalk into ¼-inch pieces. Put the pieces in the mixing bowl.

▲**4.** Place the carrot on the cutting board. Using the vegetable peeler, peel off the skin.

With the paring knife, cut off the ends. Discard the skin and ends.

Cut the carrot lengthwise in half. Place each half, flat side down, on the cutting board. Cut each half crosswise into thin slices. Put the slices in the mixing bowl.

▲**5.** Place the apple on the cutting board. With the paring knife, cut it in half lengthwise, starting at the stem end.

With the melon baller, scoop out and discard the seeds and core.

Place each half, flat side down, on the cutting board. With the paring knife, cut each half into ¼-inch slices. Put the slices in the mixing bowl.

▲**6.** Place the cheese slices, one on top of another, on the cutting board. With the paring knife, cut them crosswise into ½-inch-wide strips. Using your fingers, separate the strips and put them in the mixing bowl.

7. Add the chicken and walnuts. Using the spoon, stir the mixture until it is well combined. Serve the Chicken and Apple Salad with bagel chips.

This recipe for a crisp and fresh salad includes extra dressing. Just keep it in the refrigerator, and it's ready when you are!

Garden Salad
with Vinaigrette Dressing

15 minutes
PREPARATION

0 minutes
COOKING

15 minutes
TOTAL TIME

DEGREE OF DIFFICULTY: **EASY**
SERVINGS: **4**

UTENSILS
Cutting board
1-cup dry measuring cup
1-cup liquid measuring cup
Measuring spoons
Salad spinner or large saucepot or
    bowl and colander
Paper towels or kitchen towels
Large bowl
Paring knife
Vegetable peeler
Jar with lid
Large fork
Large spoon

INGREDIENTS

Garden Salad
4 cups packed salad greens, such as
    arugula, bibb, Boston, green leaf,
    iceberg, radicchio, red leaf, romaine,
    spinach, and watercress
2 medium-size mushrooms (about
    2 ounces)
8 large radishes
¼ large cucumber (about 2 ounces)

Basic Vinaigrette Dressing
⅓ cup red wine vinegar
¼ teaspoon salt
⅛ teaspoon pepper
¾ cup olive or vegetable oil

1. To wash the salad greens *if you have a salad spinner,* place the salad spinner, fitted with the inner basket, in the sink. Place one-third of the greens in the basket. Fill the salad spinner with enough cold water to cover the greens. Using your hands, gently swish them through the water to remove any sand or grit.

Lift out the basket to drain the greens; set the basket aside. Pour out the sandy water. Rinse the outer container to remove any sand. Reassemble the salad spinner and place the lid on top. Spin the greens until they are fairly dry.

Repeat this step until all the greens are cleaned and dried.

To wash the salad greens *if you do not have a salad spinner,* place the large saucepot or bowl in the sink. Place all the salad greens in it. Fill the saucepot with water. Using your hands, gently swish the greens through the water to remove any sand or grit. Lift out the cleaned greens and place them in the colander to drain well.

Arrange the greens between layers of paper towels or kitchen towels to dry.

2. *To prepare the Garden Salad,* tear the greens into pieces and place them in the large bowl; set the bowl aside.

▲**3.** Rinse the mushrooms and radishes with running cold water. Pat them dry.

Place the mushrooms and radishes on the cutting board. With the paring knife, cut off and discard the end of each mushroom stem.

Cut each mushroom lengthwise into thin slices. Put the slices in the bowl.

▲**4.** With the paring knife, cut off and discard the ends of each radish.

Cut each radish lengthwise in half. Put the halves in the bowl.

▲**5.** Place the cucumber on the cutting board. Using the vegetable peeler, peel off and discard the skin.

With the paring knife, cut the cucumber lengthwise in half. Place each half, flat side down, on the cutting board. Cut each half crosswise into thin slices. Put the slices in the bowl. Set the salad aside.

6. *To prepare the Basic Vinaigrette Dressing,* pour the vinegar, salt, pepper, and olive oil into the jar. Put the lid on tightly. Shake the jar until the mixture is well combined.

7. To serve, pour ¼ cup of the dressing over the salad. Using the large fork and spoon, toss, or mix, the salad until it is evenly coated with the dressing.

Refrigerate the remaining dressing. It will keep for about a week. When you use it again, you will find that it is thick and cloudy. Don't worry, the dressing has not gone bad. Olive oil becomes semi-solid when it is refrigerated and will become liquidy again once it warms up. Before using the dressing again, remember to shake the jar until the mixture is well combined.

SALAD VARIATIONS

Salads are fun to make because there are so many ways to do them and to dress them. This recipe for Green Salad with Vinaigrette Dressing is just one sample. Use it as a guide for making different salads, depending upon your mood and what is in the refrigerator.

Here is an easy rule to follow: Use ¼ cup of the Basic Vinaigrette Dressing to toss with 4 cups of salad greens and 1 cup of salad "add-ins," such as:

Avocado, cubed
Cooked broccoli
Cooked cauliflower
Yellow or red onions, sliced
Hard-cooked egg, chopped
Tomatoes, sliced
Cherry tomatoes
Red cabbage, shredded
Cooked beets, sliced
Cooked beans: black, garbanzo,
    cannellini, kidney, etc.
Carrots, sliced
Celery, sliced
Peppers, sliced
Yellow squash, sliced
Zucchini, sliced
Sprouts
Croutons
Olives, pitted
Cheese, shredded or cubed

VINAIGRETTE VARIATIONS

Substitute a different vinegar for the red wine vinegar in the Basic Vinaigrette Dressing recipe: balsamic, white wine, cider, or herb.

Then to ¼ cup of the Basic Vinaigrette Dressing recipe add:

1 teaspoon Dijon mustard for Mustard
    Vinaigrette *or*
¼ teaspoon dried herbs for Herb
    Vinaigrette *or*
¼ teaspoon chopped garlic for Garlic
    Vinaigrette

These two favorites make a winning combination with your choice of dressings.

Tuna and Potato Salad

25 minutes
PREPARATION

25 minutes
COOKING

50 minutes
TOTAL TIME

DEGREE OF DIFFICULTY: **MODERATE**
SERVINGS: **4**

UTENSILS
Cutting board
Measuring spoons
Vegetable brush
2-quart saucepan with lid
Timer
2 medium-size mixing bowls
2 forks
Paring knife
Strainer
Can opener
Spoon
Pot holders
Slotted spoon
Small plate
Colander

INGREDIENTS
4 small red potatoes (about ¾ pound)
3 tablespoons olive oil
1 tablespoon red wine vinegar or apple
    cider vinegar

1 tablespoon chopped fresh dill or
    1 teaspoon dried dillweed
1 tablespoon plus 1 teaspoon Dijon
    mustard
¼ teaspoon salt
12 medium-size cherry tomatoes
    (about ½ pound)
2 scallions
1 can solid white tuna packed in water
    (6-ounce size)

SERVING SUGGESTION
Crusty bread, rolls, or breadsticks

1. Using the vegetable brush, scrub the potatoes while rinsing them under running cold water.

▲**2.** Put the potatoes in the saucepan. Add enough water to the saucepan to cover them.

Bring the potatoes to a boil on the stove over a high heat.

Turn down the heat to low. Cover the saucepan with the lid. Set the timer and simmer the potatoes for 20 minutes.

3. While the potatoes are cooking, put the olive oil, vinegar, dill, Dijon mustard, and salt in one of the mixing bowls. With one of the forks, beat the mixture until it is well combined. Set the salad dressing aside.

4. Remove and discard any stems from the cherry tomatoes. Rinse the tomatoes and scallions with running cold water. Pat them dry. Set the scallions aside.

▲**5.** Place the tomatoes on the cutting board. With the paring knife, cut each one lengthwise in half, starting at the stem end. Put the halves in the mixing bowl with the salad dressing.

▲**6.** Place the scallions on the cutting board. With the paring knife, cut off the roots and trim off the dark green ends. Discard the roots and ends.

Cut each scallion crosswise into thin slices. Put the slices in the mixing bowl.

7. Place the strainer in the sink. Using the can opener, open the can of tuna and pour the tuna into the strainer to drain off the liquid. Using the spoon, break up the tuna into large chunks. Put the tuna in the mixing bowl.

▲**8.** When the timer for the potatoes goes off, begin testing them for doneness by piercing a piece with the other fork to see if it feels soft and tender (see pages 20–21 for complete instructions).

When the potatoes are fully cooked, turn off the heat. Place the colander in the sink. Have an adult pour the potatoes into the colander to drain the water. *Boiling water is dangerous. Do not pour the cooked potatoes into the colander yourself.*

9. Holding the handles of the colander with the pot holders, pour the potatoes into the other mixing bowl. Put the mixing bowl in the refrigerator. Set the timer and let the potatoes cool for 15 minutes, or until they are cool enough to handle.

▲ **10.** When the potatoes have cooled, place them on the cutting board. With the paring knife, cut each one lengthwise in half. Place each half, flat side down, on the cutting

board. Cut each half lengthwise in half again. Put the potato quarters in the mixing bowl with the other ingredients.

11. Using the spoon, gently stir the mixture until it is well combined.

Serve the Tuna and Potato Salad with crusty bread, rolls, or breadsticks.

LIGHT 'N' CREAMY TUNA AND POTATO SALAD

INGREDIENTS
4 small red potatoes (about ¾ pound)
½ cup plain low fat yogurt
1 tablespoon chopped fresh dill or
    1 teaspoon dried dillweed
2 teaspoons red wine vinegar
¼ teaspoon salt
12 medium-size cherry tomatoes (about
    ½ pound)
2 scallions
1 can solid white tuna packed in water
    (6-ounce size)

SERVING SUGGESTION
Crusty bread, rolls, or breadsticks

▲**1.** Follow steps 1 and 2 in the Tuna and Potato Salad recipe.

2. While the potatoes are cooking, put the yogurt, dill, vinegar, and salt in one of the mixing bowls. With the spoon, stir the mixture until it is well combined. Set the salad dressing aside.

▲**3.** Follow steps 4, 5, 6, 7, 8, 9, 10, and 11.

With this recipe you can add or subtract ingredients depending on what you like or have in the refrigerator. Use sliced turkey in place of salami. Love olives? Toss them in. Any way you make it, this salad will taste delicious!

Antipasto Pasta Salad

30 minutes
PREPARATION

15 minutes
COOKING

45 minutes
TOTAL TIME

DEGREE OF DIFFICULTY: **MODERATE**
SERVINGS: **4**

UTENSILS
Cutting board
1-cup and 4-cup liquid measuring cups
Measuring spoons
1-cup dry measuring cup
Colander
Paring knife
5-quart saucepot
Medium-size mixing bowl
2 forks or 1 fork and 1 whisk
Pot holders
Wooden spoon
Timer
Slotted spoon
Vegetable peeler
12-inch piece waxed paper
Grater

INGREDIENTS
¼ pound green beans
¼ cup olive oil
3 tablespoons red wine vinegar or white wine vinegar
2 tablespoons grated Parmesan cheese
2 tablespoons chopped fresh basil leaves or 1 teaspoon dried basil leaves
½ package (3 cups) rotelle, wagon wheel, or shell macaroni (16-ounce size)
1 large red pepper (about 8 ounces)
2 medium-size carrots (about 2 ounces each)
2 ounces sliced salami or sliced ham (about 5 slices)

SERVING SUGGESTION
Bread or breadsticks

▲**1.** Place the colander in the sink. Put the beans in the colander and rinse them under running cold water.

Place the beans on the cutting board. Put the colander back in the sink. With the paring knife or your fingers, cut or snap off and discard each stem end.

With the paring knife, cut each bean crosswise in half. Set the pieces aside.

▲**2.** Using the 4-cup liquid measuring cup, fill the saucepot with 12 cups (3 quarts) of water. Bring the water to a boil on the stove over a high heat.

3. While the water is heating, put the olive oil, vinegar, Parmesan cheese, and basil in the mixing bowl. With a fork or a whisk, beat the mixture until it is well combined. Set the salad dressing aside.

▲**4.** Once the water starts to boil, add the macaroni. Holding the handle of the saucepot with a pot holder, stir the macaroni with the wooden spoon so it will not stick together. Set the timer and cook the macaroni for 5 minutes.

▲**5.** Add the beans. Set the timer and cook the macaroni and beans for 5 minutes.

When the timer goes off, begin testing the macaroni for doneness by rinsing a piece under running cold water to cool it well and then tasting it to see if it is al dente (see page 21 for complete instructions).

When the macaroni is fully cooked, turn off the heat. Have an adult pour the macaroni and beans into the washed colander to drain the water well. *Boiling water is danger-*

ous. Do not pour the cooked macaroni and beans into the colander yourself.

6. Rinse the macaroni and beans with running cold water to cool them. Drain the water well.

▲**7.** Rinse the pepper with running cold water. Pat it dry.

Place the pepper on the cutting board. With the paring knife, cut it lengthwise in half. With the paring knife or your fingers, remove and discard the seeds and white ribs.

With the paring knife, dice each half into ½-inch pieces. Put the pieces in the mixing bowl.

▲**8.** Place the carrots on the cutting board. Using the vegetable peeler, peel off the skins.

With the paring knife, cut off the ends. Discard the skins and ends.

Place the waxed paper on the cutting board. Place the grater on the waxed paper. Rub each carrot along the side of the grater with the largest holes. *Do this slowly and carefully so that you do not scrape your knuckles. Stop when the carrot gets too small to hold.* Put the shredded carrot in the mixing bowl.

▲**9.** Place the salami slices, one on top of another, on the cutting board. With the paring knife, cut them into ½-inch-wide strips. Using your fingers, separate the strips and put them in the mixing bowl.

10. Put the macaroni and beans in the mixing bowl. Using the wooden spoon, stir the mixture until it is well combined.

Serve the salad with bread or breadsticks.

Here's a great way to dress up rice for a delicious dinner side dish with meat, poultry, or fish.

Garden Rice

 15 minutes
PREPARATION

 30 minutes
COOKING

 45 minutes
TOTAL TIME

DEGREE OF DIFFICULTY: **EASY**
SERVINGS: **6**

UTENSILS
Cutting board
½-cup, ¼-cup, and 1-cup dry
    measuring cups
Paring knife
Small mixing bowl
Plastic food storage bag
Vegetable peeler
2-quart saucepan with lid
Timer
Pot holder
Wooden spoon
Can opener
Slotted spoon
Plate
Fork

INGREDIENTS
2 scallions
1 bunch broccoli (about 1½ pounds)
1 medium-size carrot (about 2 ounces)
1 tablespoon butter or margarine
1 can chicken broth (13¾-ounce size)
¾ cup converted long-grain rice

▲ **1.** Rinse the scallions with running cold water. Pat them dry.

Place the scallions on the cutting board. With the paring knife, cut off the roots and trim off the dark green ends. Discard the roots and ends.

Cut the scallions crosswise into thin slices. Set the scallion slices aside.

▲ **2.** Rinse the broccoli with running cold water.

Place it on the cutting board. With the paring knife, cut off enough flowerets to measure 1 cup. If any are large, cut them lengthwise in half. Put the flowerets in the mixing bowl. Put the remaining broccoli in a plastic food storage bag and refrigerate it to use another day.

▲3. Place the carrot on the cutting board. Using the vegetable peeler, peel off the skin.

With the paring knife, cut off the ends. Discard the skin and ends.

Cut the carrot lengthwise in half. Place each half, flat side down, on the cutting board. Cut each half crosswise into thin slices. Put the slices in the mixing bowl.

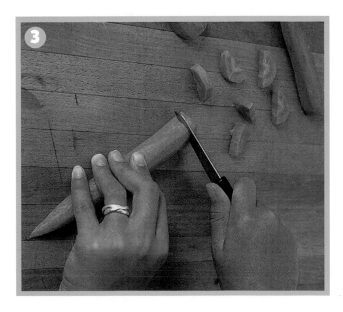

▲4. Melt the butter in the saucepan on the stove over a medium heat. Add the scallion slices. Set the timer and cook them for 2 minutes. Holding the handle of the saucepan with the pot holder, stir the slices occasionally with the wooden spoon.

▲5. Using the can opener, open the can of broth. Pour the broth into the saucepan. Bring it to a boil on the stove over a high heat.

▲6. Add the rice. Holding the handle of the saucepan with the pot holder, stir the mixture with the wooden spoon.

When the mixture begins to boil again, turn down the heat to low. Cover the saucepan with the lid. Set the timer and simmer the mixture for 20 minutes.

▲7. Add the broccoli flowerets and carrot slices. Holding the handle of the saucepan with the pot holder, stir the mixture with the wooden spoon. Cover the saucepan with the lid. Set the timer and cook the mixture for 5 minutes.

When the timer goes off, begin testing the mixture for doneness.

To test the mixture for doneness, turn off the heat. Holding the handle of the saucepan with the pot holder, use the wooden spoon to carefully remove some rice and vegetables to the plate. Set the timer and let the mixture cool for 3 minutes. Using the fork, taste the rice and vegetables to see if they are tender. If they aren't, set the timer and continue cooking for 2 minutes longer over a low heat. Then repeat this test.

When the mixture is fully cooked, the Garden Rice is ready to eat.

Crisp and brown, just like french fries, but without all the oil or trouble of frying.

Oven-Baked Potato Fries

10 minutes
PREPARATION

30 minutes
COOKING

40 minutes
TOTAL TIME

DEGREE OF DIFFICULTY: **EASY**
SERVINGS: **4**

UTENSILS
Cutting board
Measuring spoons
Vegetable brush
Paring knife
15½-inch-by-10½-inch jelly-roll pan
Rubber spatula
Pot holders
Timer
Wire rack
Pancake turner
Fork
Small plate
Serving platter

INGREDIENTS
4 baking potatoes (about 2 pounds)
1 tablespoon plus 1½ teaspoons olive
    or vegetable oil
½ teaspoon salt
½ teaspoon dried thyme leaves
¼ teaspoon pepper

▲ **1.** Preheat the oven to 450° F.

▲ **2.** Using the vegetable brush, scrub the potatoes while rinsing them under running cold water. Pat them dry.

Place the potatoes on the cutting board. With the paring knife, cut each one lengthwise in half. Place each half, flat side down, on the cutting board. Cut each half lengthwise into 3 pieces. Put the pieces in the jelly-roll pan.

3. Sprinkle the olive oil, salt, thyme, and pepper over the potatoes. Using the spatula, stir the potatoes until they are evenly coated with the olive oil and seasonings.

4. Arrange the potatoes in a single layer in the pan.

▲**5.** Using the pot holders, place the pan in the oven. Set the timer and bake the potatoes for 15 minutes.

▲**6.** Using the pot holders, remove the pan from the oven. Place it on the wire rack. Close the oven door.

▲**7.** Using a pot holder, hold one side of the pan. With the pancake turner, turn the potatoes over.

▲**8.** Using the pot holders, put the pan back in the oven. Set the timer and continue baking the potatoes for 15 minutes.

When the timer goes off, begin testing the potatoes for doneness by piercing a piece with the fork to see if it feels soft and tender (see page 21 for complete instructions). When the potatoes are fully baked, turn off the oven.

▲**9.** Using a pot holder, hold one side of the pan. With the pancake turner, place the Oven-Baked Potato Fries on the serving platter.

OVEN-BAKED SWEET POTATO FRIES

INGREDIENTS
4 sweet potatoes (about 2 pounds)
1 tablespoon plus 1½ teaspoons
    vegetable oil
½ teaspoon ground cinnamon

▲**1.** Follow steps 1 and 2 in the Oven-Baked Potato Fries recipe.

2. Sprinkle the vegetable oil and ground cinnamon over the sweet potatoes. Using the spatula, stir the sweet potatoes until they are evenly coated with the vegetable oil and seasoning.

▲**3.** Follow steps 4, 5, 6, 7, 8, and 9.

By cooking the potatoes with their skins, or jackets, on, you help keep all the fiber, iron, and minerals a potato provides.

Smashed Potatoes

10 minutes
PREPARATION

30 minutes
COOKING

40 minutes
TOTAL TIME

DEGREE OF DIFFICULTY: **EASY**

SERVINGS: **6**

UTENSILS

Cutting board
Measuring spoons
Vegetable brush
3-quart saucepan with lid
Timer
Paring knife
Pot holders
Slotted spoon
Small plate
Fork
Colander
Trivet
Potato masher
Wooden spoon

INGREDIENTS

7 medium-size red potatoes (1½ pounds)
2 scallions
4 tablespoons (½ stick) butter or
    margarine, softened
¼ teaspoon salt
⅛ teaspoon pepper

1. Using the vegetable brush, scrub the potatoes while rinsing them under running cold water.

▲**2.** Put the potatoes in the saucepan. Add enough water to cover them. Bring the potatoes to a boil on the stove over a high heat.

Turn down the heat to low and cover the saucepan with the lid. Set the timer and simmer the potatoes for 25 minutes.

▲**3.** While the potatoes are cooking, rinse the scallions with running cold water. Pat them dry. Place the scallions on the cutting board. With the paring knife, cut off the roots and trim off the dark green ends. Discard the roots and ends.

Cut each scallion crosswise into thin slices. Set the slices aside.

▲**4.** When the timer for the potatoes goes off, begin testing them for doneness by piercing a piece with the fork to see if it feels soft and tender (see pages 20–21 for complete instructions).

When the potatoes are fully cooked, turn off the heat. Place the colander in the sink. Have an adult pour the potatoes into the colander to drain the water. *Boiling water is dangerous. Do not pour the cooked potatoes into the colander yourself.*

▲**5.** Holding the handles of the colander with the pot holders, put the potatoes back in the saucepan.

▲**6.** Holding the handle of the saucepan with the pot holder, put the saucepan on the trivet. Using the potato masher, mash the potatoes coarsely, leaving large pieces of potato.

7. Add the scallions, butter, salt, and pepper.

▲**8.** Holding the handle of the saucepan with the pot holder, place the saucepan on the stove over a low heat. Still holding the handle of the saucepan with the pot holder, stir the mixture with the wooden spoon until the butter melts and the mixture is well combined. Turn off the heat.

Warm and tasty, a big bowl of fluffy mashed potatoes goes great with almost any dinner.

Mashed Potatoes

15 minutes
PREPARATION

30 minutes
COOKING

45 minutes
TOTAL TIME

DEGREE OF DIFFICULTY: **MODERATE**

SERVINGS: **4**

UTENSILS

Cutting board
1-cup liquid measuring cup
Measuring spoons
Vegetable peeler
Paring knife
3-quart saucepan with lid
Timer
Pot holders
Slotted spoon
Small plate
Fork
Colander
Trivet
Potato masher
Wooden spoon

INGREDIENTS

4 large all-purpose or Russet potatoes
    (about 2 pounds)
½ cup milk
3 tablespoons butter or margarine,
    softened
½ teaspoon salt
⅛ teaspoon pepper

▲ **1.** Place the potatoes on the cutting board. Using the vegetable peeler, peel off and discard the skins. Rinse the potatoes with running cold water.

Place the potatoes on the cutting board. With the paring knife, cut each one lengthwise in half. Place each half, flat side down, on the cutting board. Cut each half crosswise into 1-inch slices.

2. Put the potato slices in the saucepan. Add enough water to cover them.

▲ **3.** Bring the potatoes to a boil on the stove over a high heat.

Turn down the heat to low. Cover the saucepan with the lid. Set the timer and simmer the potatoes for 15 minutes.

When the timer goes off, begin testing the potatoes for doneness by piercing a piece with the fork to see if it feels soft and tender (see pages 20–21 for complete instructions).

When the potatoes are fully cooked, place the colander in the sink. Have an adult pour the potatoes into the colander to drain the water. *Boiling water is dangerous. Do not pour the cooked potatoes into the colander yourself.*

▲ **4.** Holding the handles of the colander with the pot holders, put the potatoes back into the saucepan.

▲ **5.** Holding the handle of the saucepan with the pot holder, put the saucepan on the trivet. Using the potato masher, mash the potatoes until they are smooth.

6. Add the milk, butter, salt, and pepper.

▲ **7.** Holding the handle of the saucepan with the pot holder, place the saucepan on the stove over a low heat. Still holding the handle of the saucepan with the pot holder, stir the mixture with the wooden spoon until it is well combined and hot. Turn off the heat.

HINT: If you need to reheat the mashed potatoes, stir in a little extra milk.

MASHED SWEET POTATOES AND APPLE

UTENSILS
Cutting board
Measuring spoons
Vegetable peeler
Paring knife
Melon baller
3-quart saucepan with lid
Timer
Pot holders
Slotted spoon
Small plate
Fork
Colander
Trivet
Potato masher
Wooden spoon

INGREDIENTS
3 large sweet potatoes (about 1½
    pounds)
1 large red cooking apple, such as
    McIntosh or Rome Beauty (8 ounces)
3 tablespoons butter or margarine,
    softened
1 tablespoon packed brown sugar
¼ teaspoon salt
¼ teaspoon ground cinnamon

▲ **1.** Follow step 1 in the Mashed Potatoes recipe.

2. Put the sweet potatoes in the saucepan. Set the saucepan aside.

▲ **3.** Place the apple on the cutting board.

Using the vegetable peeler, peel off and discard the skin.

With the paring knife, cut the apple in half lengthwise, starting at the stem end.

With the melon baller, scoop out and discard the seeds and core.

Place each half, flat side down, on the cutting board. With the paring knife, cut each half into 2-inch pieces.

4. Put the apple pieces in the saucepan with the potatoes. Add enough water to cover them.

▲ **5.** Follow step 3, but do not cover the saucepan with the lid.

▲ **6.** Follow steps 4 and 5.

7. Add the butter, brown sugar, salt, and cinnamon.

▲ **8.** Follow step 7.

It's fun to arrange these vegetables in layers in the casserole. Just wait until they come out of the oven tender and golden with a crunchy bread topping.

Layered Vegetable Bake

25 minutes   45 minutes
PREPARATION   COOKING

1 hour 10 minutes
TOTAL TIME

DEGREE OF DIFFICULTY: **DIFFICULT**
SERVINGS: **4 to 6**

UTENSILS
Cutting board
¼-cup dry measuring cup
Measuring spoons
Small mixing bowl
Paring knife
Spoon
Vegetable brush
1½-quart casserole
Aluminum foil
Pot holders
Timer
Trivet

INGREDIENTS
¼ loaf Italian bread (2 ounces)
1 clove garlic
¼ cup grated Parmesan cheese
1 tablespoon olive oil
1 medium-size zucchini (8 ounces)
1 small tomato (4 ounces)
4 small red potatoes (about ½ pound)
Nonstick cooking spray
½ teaspoon salt
½ teaspoon dried thyme leaves
Pepper

1. With your fingers, tear the bread into ¼-inch pieces, or coarse bread crumbs. Put them in the mixing bowl.

▲**2.** Place the garlic clove on the cutting board. With the paring knife, cut off the stem end. With the paring knife or your fingers, peel off the skin. Discard the end and skin.

With the paring knife, chop the garlic clove. Put the pieces in the mixing bowl.

3. Add the Parmesan cheese and olive oil. With the spoon, stir the mixture until it is well combined. Set the bread crumb mixture aside.

▲**4.** Preheat the oven to 400° F.

5. With the vegetable brush, scrub the zucchini while rinsing it under running cold water. Rinse the tomato under running cold water. Pat them dry. Set the tomato aside.

▲**6.** Place the zucchini on the cutting board. With the paring knife, cut off and discard the ends.

Cut the zucchini crosswise into ¼-inch slices. Set the slices aside.

▲**7.** Place the tomato on the cutting board. With the paring knife, remove and discard the core.

Cut the tomato into thin slices. Set the slices aside.

▲**8.** With the vegetable brush, scrub the potatoes while rinsing them under running cold water. Pat them dry.

Place the potatoes on the cutting board. With the paring knife, cut each one crosswise into ¼-inch slices. Set the slices aside.

9. Lightly spray the casserole with the nonstick cooking spray.

10. Place the potato slices in circles to cover the bottom of the casserole. You can overlap them slightly to fit them in the casserole.

11. Sprinkle the potato layer with ¼ teaspoon of salt, ¼ teaspoon of thyme, and a pinch of pepper.

12. Place the zucchini slices in circles to cover the potato layer. You can overlap them slightly, if necessary.

16. If the casserole *comes with a lid,* cover it with the lid.

If the casserole *does not come with a lid,* tear off a piece of aluminum foil. Place the foil over the casserole and fold the edges of the foil over the edge of the casserole to seal it.

13. Sprinkle the zucchini layer with ¼ teaspoon of salt, ¼ teaspoon of thyme, and a pinch of pepper.

14. Place the tomato slices in a circle in the center of the casserole on top of the zucchini layer. You can overlap them slightly.

▲ **17.** Using the pot holders, place the casserole in the oven. Set the timer and bake the vegetables for 40 minutes.

When the timer goes off, begin testing the vegetables for doneness by piercing the potatoes with a paring knife to see if they feel soft (see page 21 for complete instructions).

▲ **18.** When the vegetables are fully cooked, using the pot holders, put the uncovered casserole back in the oven. Set the timer and continue baking for 5 minutes, or until the bread crumb mixture is golden brown.

▲ **19.** Using the pot holders, remove the casserole from the oven and place it on the trivet. Turn off the oven.

Serve the Layered Vegetable Bake as a side dish with meat or poultry.

15. Sprinkle the bread crumb mixture on top.

Drinks and Desserts

◆ ◆ ◆ ◆ ◆ ◆ ◆ ◆ ◆ ◆ ◆ ◆ ◆ ◆

A refreshing combination of mint-flavored tea and tropical fruit juice, this thirst-quenching drink doesn't contain caffeine.

Fruited Ice Tea

15 minutes
PREPARATION

10 minutes
COOKING

2 hours
CHILLING/
FREEZING TIME

2 hours 25 minutes
TOTAL TIME

DEGREE OF DIFFICULTY: **EASY**
SERVINGS: **6**

UTENSILS
Cutting board
1-cup liquid measuring cup
Measuring spoons
Paring knife
Ice cube tray
Tea kettle
Large metal mixing bowl
Pot holder
2-cup liquid measuring cup
Timer
Spoon
Plastic wrap
Glasses
Ladle

INGREDIENTS

Fruited Ice Cubes
7 small strawberries (about 3 ounces)
14 mint leaves (optional)
1 cup refrigerated tropical fruit juice blend

Fruited Ice Tea
Water
2 caffeine-free mint-flavored herbal tea bags
2 tablespoons sugar
4 cups refrigerated tropical fruit juice blend

▲ **1.** *To prepare the Fruited Ice Cubes,* rinse the strawberries with running cold water. Pat them dry.

Place them on the cutting board. With the paring knife, remove and discard the stems.

Cut each strawberry lengthwise in half.

2. Place a strawberry half and a mint leaf in each compartment of the ice cube tray.

Pour the fruit juice into the ice cube tray. Place the tray in the freezer for 2 hours, or until the ice cubes freeze.

3. While the ice cubes are freezing, prepare the Fruited Ice Tea.

▲ **4.** *To prepare the Fruited Ice Tea,* fill the tea kettle half full with water. Bring the water to a boil on the stove over a high heat.

▲ **5.** Place the tea bags in the mixing bowl.

When the water has come to a boil, turn off the heat. Have an adult fill the 2-cup liquid measuring cup with boiling water and pour it over the tea bags. *Boiling water is dangerous. Do not pour the water into the measuring cup or over the tea bags yourself.*

▲ **6.** Set the timer and steep the tea for 5 minutes. Using the spoon, remove and discard the tea bags.

▲ **7.** Add the sugar. Stir the tea with the spoon until the sugar dissolves completely. Add the fruit juice. Stir the tea with the spoon.

8. Cover the mixing bowl with plastic wrap. Place it in the refrigerator to chill the tea.

To serve, place some Fruited Ice Cubes in each glass. Using the ladle, pour some Fruited Ice Tea into each glass.

HINT: You can make this recipe with plain ice cubes or no ice cubes at all. Just eliminate the Fruited Ice Cubes ingredients.

Great for chasing the cold away, this recipe can easily be halved or doubled.

Orangy Hot Chocolate

5 minutes
PREPARATION

10 minutes
COOKING

15 minutes
TOTAL TIME

DEGREE OF DIFFICULTY: **EASY**
SERVINGS: **2**

UTENSILS
Cutting board
2-cup liquid measuring cup
¼-cup dry measuring cup
Vegetable peeler
Ruler
1-quart saucepan
Pot holder
Wooden spoon
Tongs
Mugs or cups

INGREDIENTS
1 orange
2 cups milk or low fat milk (1 percent)
¼ cup sweetened chocolate powder

SERVING SUGGESTION
Whipped cream (see recipe on pages 141 and 143) or 2 marshmallows

▲ **1.** Wash the orange with running cold water. Pat it dry.

Place it on the cutting board. Using the vegetable peeler, remove four strips of orange peel, each about 4 inches long and 1 inch wide. Place the strips in the saucepan.

▲ **2.** Pour the milk into the saucepan. Heat the milk on the stove over a medium heat until tiny bubbles form around the edge.

▲ **3.** Add the chocolate powder. Holding the handle of the saucepan with the pot holder, stir the milk with the wooden spoon until the powder dissolves. Turn off the heat.

▲ **4.** Holding the handle of the saucepan with the pot holder, use the tongs to remove and discard the orange peels.

Pour the hot chocolate into the mugs. Top each serving with some whipped cream or a marshmallow, if you like.

This nutritious drink is great at breakfast or as an after-school snack.

Smoothies

BANANA SMOOTHIE

10 minutes	0 minutes	10 minutes
PREPARATION	COOKING	TOTAL TIME

DEGREE OF DIFFICULTY: **EASY**

SERVINGS: **2**

UTENSILS
Cutting board
1-cup liquid measuring cup
Rubber spatula
Blender
Paring knife
Timer

INGREDIENTS
1 container vanilla low fat yogurt
    (8-ounce size)
¾ cup pineapple or orange juice
1 large ripe banana (about 7 ounces)

1. Using the spatula, scrape out the yogurt into the blender container.

2. Add the pineapple juice.

▲**3.** Place the banana on the cutting board. Peel off and discard the skin. With the knife, cut the banana crosswise into 4 pieces. Put the pieces in the blender container.

▲**4.** Press the lid of the blender firmly into place. Set the timer and blend the mixture on medium speed for 1 minute, or until it is smooth. Turn off the blender. *Wait until the blender blades have completely stopped; then remove the lid and serve.*

STRAWBERRY SMOOTHIE

ADDITIONAL UTENSILS
1- and 1½-cup dry measuring cups
Measuring spoons

INGREDIENTS
1 container vanilla low fat yogurt
    (8-ounce size)
1½ cups strawberries (about 6¾ ounces)
2 teaspoons sugar
4 ice cubes

1. Follow step 1 in the Banana Smoothie recipe and omit steps 2 and 3.

▲**2.** Rinse the strawberries with running cold water. Pat them dry.
    Place them on the cutting board. With the paring knife, remove and discard the stems. Cut each strawberry in half. Put the halves in the blender container.
    Add the sugar and the ice cubes.

▲**3.** Follow step 4.

A delicious recipe that combines cinnamon-scented apples with a crunchy topping. It's a great dessert or snack.

Apple-Cherry Crisp

 30 minutes
PREPARATION

 50 minutes
COOKING

 1 hour 20 minutes
TOTAL TIME

DEGREE OF DIFFICULTY: **EASY**

SERVINGS: **6**

UTENSILS

Cutting board
½-cup, ⅓-cup, and ¼-cup dry
  measuring cups
Measuring spoons
Medium-size mixing bowl
Wooden spoon
Vegetable peeler
Paring knife
Melon baller
1½-quart round casserole
Pot holders
Timer
Cooling rack
Fork
Serving spoon
Dessert plates

INGREDIENTS

½ cup quick-cooking oats, uncooked
⅓ cup pecan pieces
¼ cup all-purpose flour
¼ cup packed brown sugar
½ teaspoon ground cinnamon
4 tablespoons (½ stick) butter or
  margarine, softened

4 large red cooking apples, such as
    McIntosh or Rome Beauty
    (2 pounds)
½ cup dried cherries, raisins, or dried
    cranberries

SERVING SUGGESTION
Vanilla ice cream or vanilla frozen yogurt

1. Pour the oats, pecans, flour, brown sugar, and cinnamon into the mixing bowl. With the wooden spoon, stir the oat mixture until it is well combined.

2. Add the butter. Rub the oat and butter mixture between your fingertips until it is well blended.

▲ **3.** Preheat the oven to 375° F.

▲ **4.** Place the apples on the cutting board. Using the vegetable peeler, peel off and dis-

card the skins. With the paring knife, cut each apple in half lengthwise, starting at the stem end. With the melon baller, scoop out and discard the seeds and cores.

Place each half, flat side down, on the cutting board. With the paring knife, cut each half into thin slices. Put the slices in the casserole.

5. Add the dried cherries. With the wooden spoon, stir the mixture until the apple slices and cherries are well combined.

Sprinkle the oat and butter mixture on top.

▲ **6.** Using the pot holders, place the casserole in the oven. Set the timer and bake the crisp for 50 minutes.

When the timer goes off, begin testing the crisp for doneness.

To test the crisp for doneness, using the pot holders, carefully remove the casserole from the oven and place it on the cooling rack. Close the oven door. Holding a side of the casserole with a pot holder, use the fork to pierce the apple mixture in several places to see if the apples feel soft. If they don't, using the pot holders, carefully put the casserole back into the oven. Set the timer and continue baking for 5 minutes longer. Then repeat this test. When the crisp is fully baked, turn off the oven.

Serve the Apple-Cherry Crisp warm or at room temperature.

To serve the crisp warm, let it cool for about 15 minutes. Then, holding a side of the casserole with a pot holder, use the serving spoon to scoop out some crisp onto each dessert plate. Top it with vanilla ice cream or vanilla frozen yogurt, if you like.

This delicious bread can be served as a snack, as a dessert, or for breakfast.

Tropical Banana Bread

50 minutes
PREPARATION

1 hour
COOKING

1 hour 50 minutes
TOTAL TIME

DEGREE OF DIFFICULTY: **EASY**

SERVINGS: **12**

UTENSILS
Cutting board
1-cup, ½-cup, ¼-cup, and ⅓-cup dry
    measuring cups
Measuring spoons
9-inch-by-5-inch loaf pan
12-inch piece waxed paper
Grater
Plastic wrap
2 medium-size mixing bowls
Fork or potato masher
Wooden spoon
Electric mixer with large bowl
Small bowl or cup
Rubber spatula
Pot holders
Timer
Cooling rack
Wooden skewer
Table knife

INGREDIENTS
Nonstick cooking spray
1 orange (about 8 ounces)
2 large ripe bananas (1 pound)
1 cup all-purpose flour
¾ cup whole wheat flour
2 teaspoons baking powder
½ teaspoon salt
½ cup (1 stick) butter or margarine,
    softened
⅔ cup sugar
2 large eggs
¾ cup shredded coconut
½ cup pecan pieces

SERVING SUGGESTION
Cream cheese

▲ **1.** Preheat the oven to 350° F.

2. Spray the pan with nonstick cooking spray; set it aside.

▲**3.** Wash the orange with running cold water. Pat it dry.

Place the waxed paper on the cutting board. Place the grater on the waxed paper. Rub the orange along the side of the grater with the medium-size holes. *Do this slowly and carefully so that you do not scrape your knuckles.* Also, rub gently so that you remove only the orange skin, not the bitter white pith beneath it. Grate enough peel to measure 1 teaspoon. Wrap the orange in plastic wrap, and refrigerate it to eat or use another day.

4. Place the bananas on the cutting board. Peel off and discard the skins. Put the bananas in one of the mixing bowls. Using the fork, mash them until they are smooth. Set them aside.

5. Pour the all-purpose flour, whole wheat flour, baking powder, and salt into the other mixing bowl. With the wooden spoon, stir the flour mixture until it is well combined.

▲**6.** Put the butter and sugar in the mixer bowl. With the mixer set at low speed, beat the mixture just until it is blended and creamy. Turn off the mixer.

▲**7.** Crack the eggs into the small bowl; discard the shells.

Put the cracked eggs and grated orange peel in the mixer bowl. With the mixer set at low speed, beat the mixture until it is well combined. Turn off the mixer.

▲**8.** Using the spatula, scrape the mashed banana into the mixer bowl. With the mixer set at low speed, beat the mixture until it is well combined. Turn off the mixer.

▲**9.** Add the flour mixture. With the mixer set at low speed, beat the mixture. Occasionally turn off the mixer and scrape down the side of the mixer bowl with the spatula. When the batter is well combined, turn off the mixer.

10. Pour the coconut and pecans into the mixer bowl. Using the wooden spoon, stir the batter until the coconut and pecans are well combined.

11. Using the wooden spoon, spoon the batter evenly into the pan. Using the spatula, scrape up all the batter from the mixer bowl and add it to the pan.

▲**12.** Using the pot holders, place the pan in the oven. Set the timer and bake the bread for 1 hour.

When the timer goes off, begin testing the bread for doneness by inserting the wooden skewer into the center of the bread to see if it comes out clean (see pages 21–22 for complete instructions). When the bread is fully baked, turn off the oven.

Set the timer and let the bread cool for 10 minutes.

▲**13.** Holding a side of the pan with a pot holder, run the table knife around the edge of the bread to loosen it from the pan. Holding the pan with both pot holders, turn it over and let the bread fall out onto the cooling rack. Using the pot holders, turn the bread right side up. Let it cool completely.

Tropical Banana Bread is delicious served with cream cheese, and it tastes even better when it's prepared a day ahead.

Fudgy and moist, these brownies are studded with chocolate chips and nuts.

Double Chocolate Brownies

20 minutes
PREPARATION

35 minutes
COOKING

55 minutes
TOTAL TIME

DEGREE OF DIFFICULTY: **EASY**

YIELD: **16 brownies**

UTENSILS

Cutting board

½-cup, ¼-cup, and ⅓-cup dry
    measuring cups

Measuring spoons

9-inch-by-9-inch baking pan

Medium-size mixing bowl

Wooden spoon

Electric mixer with large bowl

Timer

Rubber spatula

Small bowl or cup

Pot holders

Cooling rack

Wooden skewer

Paring knife

Pancake turner

Serving plate

INGREDIENTS

Nonstick cooking spray
¾ cup all-purpose flour
⅓ cup unsweetened cocoa powder
½ teaspoon salt
½ teaspoon baking powder
½ cup (1 stick) butter or margarine, softened
1 cup sugar
2 large eggs
1 teaspoon vanilla extract
½ cup semisweet chocolate morsels
½ cup walnut pieces (optional)

▲1. Preheat the oven to 350° F.

2. Spray the baking pan with nonstick cooking spray; set the pan aside.

3. Pour the flour, cocoa powder, salt, and baking powder into the mixing bowl. With the wooden spoon, stir the flour mixture until it is well combined.

▲4. Put the butter and sugar in the mixer bowl. Set the timer for 5 minutes. With the mixer set at medium speed, beat the mixture. Occasionally turn off the mixer and scrape down the side of the mixer bowl with the spatula. When the timer goes off, or when the mixture is light and fluffy, turn off the mixer.

▲5. Crack the eggs into the small bowl; discard the shells.

Add the cracked eggs and vanilla extract to the mixer bowl. With the mixer set at low speed, beat the mixture until it is well combined. Turn off the mixer.

▲6. Add the flour mixture. With the mixer set at low speed, beat the mixture. Occasionally turn off the mixer and scrape down the side of the mixer bowl with the spatula. When the batter is well combined, turn off the mixer.

7. Pour the chocolate morsels and walnuts into the mixer bowl. Using the wooden spoon, stir the batter until the chocolate morsels and walnuts are well combined.

8. Using the wooden spoon, spoon the batter evenly into the pan. Using the spatula, scrape up all the batter from the mixer bowl and add it to the pan.

▲9. Using the pot holders, place the pan in the oven. Set the timer and bake the brownies for 35 minutes.

When the timer goes off, begin testing the brownies for doneness by inserting the wooden skewer into the center of the brownies to see if it comes out clean (see pages 21–22 for complete instructions). When the brownies are fully baked, turn off the oven.

▲10. Let the brownies cool completely. Then, holding a side of the pan, run the paring knife around the edge of the brownies to loosen them from the pan. Cut the brownies into 16 equal pieces. Using the pancake turner, remove the brownies one at a time. Place the brownies on the serving plate.

Store any Double Chocolate Brownies that are left in a tightly covered container with a sheet of waxed paper between each layer of brownies.

Buttery, crunchy, and full of chocolate. No wonder chocolate chip cookies are everyone's favorite!

Chocolate Chip Cookies

30 minutes
PREPARATION

9 minutes
per cookie sheet
COOKING

1 hour 25 minutes
TOTAL TIME

DEGREE OF DIFFICULTY: **MODERATE**
YIELD: **ABOUT 6 DOZEN COOKIES**

UTENSILS

Cutting board
1-cup, ½-cup, and ¼-cup dry
    measuring cups
Measuring spoons
Medium-size mixing bowl
Wooden spoon
Electric mixer with large bowl
Small bowl or cup
Rubber spatula
Thin rubber spatula or spoon
Large cookie sheet
Ruler
Pot holders
Timer
2 cooling racks
Pancake turner

INGREDIENTS

2 cups all-purpose flour
1½ cups quick-cooking oats, uncooked
1 teaspoon baking soda
1 teaspoon salt
1 cup (2 sticks) butter or margarine,
    softened
¾ cup sugar
¾ cup packed brown sugar
2 large eggs
1 teaspoon vanilla extract
1 package semisweet chocolate pieces
    (12-ounce size)
1 cup walnut pieces

▲ **1.** Preheat the oven to 375° F.

2. Pour the flour, oats, baking soda, and salt into the mixing bowl. With the wooden spoon, stir the flour mixture until it is well combined.

▲3. Put the butter, sugar, and brown sugar in the mixer bowl. With the mixer set at low speed, beat the mixture until it is well blended and creamy. Turn off the mixer.

▲4. Crack the eggs into the small bowl; discard the shells.

Add the cracked eggs and vanilla extract to the mixer bowl. With the mixer set at low speed, beat the mixture until it is well combined. Turn off the mixer.

▲5. Add the flour mixture. With the mixer set at low speed, beat the mixture. Occasionally turn off the mixer and scrape down the side of the mixer bowl with the spatula. When the dough is well combined, turn off the mixer.

6. Pour the chocolate pieces and walnuts into the mixer bowl. Using the wooden spoon, stir the dough until the chocolate pieces and walnuts are well combined.

7. Using the tablespoon measuring spoon, scoop up enough dough to make a rounded spoonful. Using the thin spatula, scrape the dough out of the measuring spoon and drop it onto the cookie sheet.

Repeat this step, dropping rounded tablespoonfuls of dough about 2 inches apart, until the cookie sheet is full.

▲8. Using the pot holders, place the cookie sheet in the oven. Set the timer and bake the cookies for 9 minutes.

When the timer goes off, begin testing the cookies for doneness by seeing if they are golden brown (see page 22 for complete instructions).

When the cookies are fully baked, using the pot holders, remove the cookie sheet from the oven and place it on a cooling rack. Close the oven door. Set the timer and let the cookies cool for 5 minutes.

▲9. Holding an end of the cookie sheet with a pot holder, use the pancake turner to remove the cookies one at a time. Place the cookies on the other cooling rack in a single layer to cool completely.

▲10. Set the timer and let the cookie sheet cool completely, for about 15 minutes. Wash the cookie sheet and then repeat steps 7, 8, 9, and 10 until all the dough is used. When you have finished baking all the cookies, turn off the oven.

Store any Chocolate Chip Cookies that are left in a tightly covered container.

Do you like your cookies plain or fancy?

Peanut Butter Cookies

45 minutes
to 1 hour
PREPARATION

10 minutes
per cookie sheet
COOKING

Approximately 1 hour 40 minutes
TOTAL TIME

DEGREE OF DIFFICULTY: **MODERATE**
YIELD: **ABOUT 4 DOZEN COOKIES**

UTENSILS

Cutting board
1-cup, ½-cup, and ¼-cup dry
    measuring cups
Measuring spoons
Medium-size mixing bowl
Wooden spoon
Electric mixer with large bowl
Small bowl or cup
Rubber spatula
Large cookie sheet
Ruler
Small plate
Wide-bottomed glass
Spoon
Pot holders
Timer
2 cooling racks
Pancake turner

INGREDIENTS

1½ cups all-purpose flour
1 teaspoon baking soda
¼ teaspoon salt
½ cup (1 stick) butter or margarine,
    softened
½ cup packed brown sugar
¼ cup plus 2 teaspoons sugar
1 large egg
1 cup creamy peanut butter
½ teaspoon vanilla extract
Nonstick cooking spray
About ¾ cup grape jelly (optional)

1. Pour the flour, baking soda, and salt into the mixing bowl. With the wooden spoon, stir the flour mixture until it is well combined.

▲**2.** Put the butter, brown sugar, and ¼ cup of sugar in the mixer bowl. With the mixer set at low speed, beat the mixture until it is well blended and creamy. Turn off the mixer.

▲**3.** Crack the egg into the small bowl; discard the shells.

Add the cracked egg, peanut butter, and vanilla extract to the mixer bowl. With the mixer set at low speed, beat the mixture until it is well combined. Turn off the mixer.

▲ **4.** Add the flour mixture. With the mixer set at low speed, beat the mixture. Occasionally turn off the mixer and scrape down the side of the mixer bowl with the spatula. When the batter is well combined, turn off the mixer.

▲ **5.** Preheat the oven to 375° F.

6. Using your hands, break off a small piece of dough and shape it into a 1-inch ball. Place the ball on the cookie sheet.

Repeat this step, placing the balls of dough about 2 inches apart, until the cookie sheet is full.

7. Pour the remaining 2 teaspoons of sugar into the small plate.

Lightly spray the bottom of the glass with nonstick cooking spray. Dip the glass into the sugar. Using the bottom of the glass, flatten each ball of dough into a 2-inch round. If the dough begins to stick to the bottom of the glass, dip the glass into the sugar again.

8. If you like your peanut butter cookies *plain,* then follow steps 9, 10, and 11.

If you like your peanut butter cookies *with jelly,* using the tip of your index finger, make a slight well in the center of each cookie. Using the spoon, stir the jelly until it is smooth. Using the ¼-teaspoon measuring spoon, spoon some jelly into each well. Then follow steps 9, 10, and 11.

▲ **9.** Using the pot holders, place the cookie sheet in the oven. Set the timer and bake the cookies for 10 minutes.

When the timer goes off, begin testing the cookies for doneness by seeing if they are golden brown (see page 22 for complete instructions).

When the cookies are fully baked, using the pot holders, remove the cookie sheet from the oven and place it on a cooling rack. Close the oven door. Set the timer and let the cookies cool for 5 minutes.

▲ **10.** Holding an end of the cookie sheet with a pot holder, use the pancake turner to remove the cookies one at a time. Place the cookies on the other cooling rack in a single layer to cool completely.

▲ **11.** Set the timer and let the cookie sheet cool completely, about 15 minutes. Wash the cookie sheet and then repeat steps 6, 7, 8, 9, 10, and 11 until all the dough is used. When you have finished baking all the cookies, turn off the oven.

Store any Peanut Butter Cookies that are left in a tightly covered container with a sheet of waxed paper between each layer of cookies.

This cake is like two desserts in one. While the batter bakes, it magically separates into a cake layer that sits on top of a luscious chocolaty sauce.

Chocolate Pudding Cake

 25 minutes
PREPARATION

 30 minutes
COOKING

 55 minutes
TOTAL TIME

DEGREE OF DIFFICULTY: **MODERATE**

SERVINGS: **6**

UTENSILS

Cutting board
1-cup, ½-cup, and ¼-cup dry
    measuring cups
Measuring spoons
2-cup liquid measuring cup
8-inch-by-8-inch baking pan
Large mixing bowl
Wooden spoon
Small mixing bowl
Rubber spatula
Pot holders
Timer
Cooling rack
Serving spoon
Dessert plates

INGREDIENTS

Nonstick cooking spray
1 cup all-purpose flour
¾ cup sugar
2 teaspoons baking powder
½ teaspoon salt
¾ cup unsweetened cocoa powder
½ cup packed brown sugar
½ cup milk
¼ cup (½ stick) butter, melted
2 teaspoons vanilla extract
½ cup walnut or pecan pieces
1¾ cups hot tap water

SERVING SUGGESTION

Whipped cream (see recipe on pages 141 and 143), vanilla ice cream, or vanilla frozen yogurt

▲**1.** Preheat the oven to 350° F.

2. Spray the baking pan with nonstick cooking spray; set the baking pan aside.

3. Pour the flour, sugar, baking powder, salt, and ½ cup of the cocoa powder into the large mixing bowl. With the wooden spoon, stir the flour mixture until it is well combined.

4. Pour the remaining ¼ cup of cocoa powder and the brown sugar into the small mixing bowl. With the wooden spoon, stir the cocoa powder mixture until it is well combined.

5. Add the milk, melted butter, and vanilla extract to the flour mixture. With the wooden spoon, stir the batter until it is smooth and well combined. Add the nuts. Stir the batter until the nuts are well combined.

6. Spoon the batter evenly into the baking pan. Using the spatula, scrape up all the batter from the mixing bowl and add it to the baking pan.

▲**7.** Sprinkle the cocoa powder mixture evenly on top.

Slowly pour the hot water over the cocoa powder mixture.

▲**8.** Using the pot holders, place the baking pan in the oven. Set the timer and bake the cake for 30 minutes.

When the timer goes off, begin testing the cake for doneness.

To test the cake for doneness, using the pot holders, carefully pull out the oven rack that the baking pan is on and see if the top looks dry, not unbaked, and the edges are bubbly. If the top is not dry looking, using the pot holders, carefully push the oven rack back into the oven. Set the timer and continue baking for 5 minutes longer. Then repeat this test.

When the cake is fully baked, turn off the oven. Using the pot holders, remove the baking pan from the oven and place it on the cooling rack. Close the oven door.

▲**9.** Serve the Chocolate Pudding Cake warm.

To serve, let it cool for about 20 minutes. Then, holding a side of the baking pan with a pot holder, use the serving spoon to scoop out some cake onto each dessert plate. Top it with whipped cream, vanilla ice cream, or vanilla frozen yogurt, if you like.

Rich, flaky biscuits are topped with lightly sweetened fruit and a mound of whipped cream. The perfect way to end a meal!

Shortcake

55 minutes
PREPARATION

15 minutes
COOKING

1 hour 10 minutes
TOTAL TIME

DEGREE OF DIFFICULTY: **MODERATE**
SERVINGS: **4**

UTENSILS

Cutting board
Measuring spoons
1-cup dry measuring cup
1-cup liquid measuring cup
Cookie sheet
2 medium-size mixing bowls
Wooden spoon
Pastry blender
Fork
Ruler
3-inch heart-shaped cookie cutter
      or 2 ¾-inch round cookie cutter
Pastry brush

Pot holders
Timer
Paring knife
Vegetable peeler
Spoon
Electric mixer with small bowl
2 cooling racks
Pancake turner
Dessert plates

INGREDIENTS

Nonstick cooking spray

Biscuits

2 teaspoons baking powder
¼ teaspoon salt
1 cup plus 1 tablespoon all-purpose flour
1 tablespoon plus 1 teaspoon sugar
5 tablespoons cold butter, cut into small pieces
⅓ cup plus 1 tablespoon milk

Fruit Filling

1 cup strawberries (about 5 ounces)
2 medium-size peaches or nectarines
    (about 10 ounces)
1 tablespoon sugar

Whipped Cream

½ cup heavy cream
½ teaspoon vanilla extract
1½ teaspoons sugar

▲ **1.** Preheat the oven to 375° F.

2. Spray the cookie sheet with the nonstick cooking spray and set the cookie sheet aside.

3. *To prepare the biscuits,* pour the baking powder, salt, 1 cup of flour, and 1 tablespoon of sugar into one of the mixing bowls. With the wooden spoon, stir the flour mixture until it is well combined. Add the pieces of butter.

4. If you *have a pastry blender,* cut the butter into smaller and smaller pieces until it combines with the flour mixture and looks like coarse crumbs.

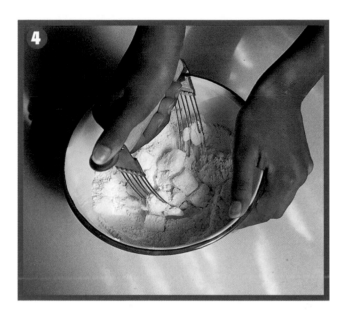

If you *do not have a pastry blender,* quickly rub the pieces of butter and the flour mixture between your fingertips until coarse crumbs are formed.

5. Add ⅓ cup of milk. Using the fork, stir the mixture until it is well combined. A soft dough that will leave the side of the bowl will form as you stir the mixture. With your hand, gather the dough up into a ball.

6. Sprinkle a small area on the cutting board with the remaining 1 tablespoon of flour.

Place the dough on the floured section of the cutting board. Using your hands, knead the dough 10 times, or until it is smooth.

7. Starting from the center of the dough and moving out, use your hands to pat the dough gently into a circle that measures about 7 inches across and ½ inch thick.

8. Starting from the edge of the dough, push the cookie cutter straight down into the dough to cut it. Do not twist the cutter. Place the cutter next to the cut-out section of dough and repeat this step until you have cut the dough into 4 biscuits.

9. Place the biscuits on the cookie sheet. Dip the pastry brush into the small bowl containing the remaining 1 tablespoon of milk. Brush the top of each biscuit to coat it with milk.

Sprinkle some of the remaining 1 teaspoon of sugar on top of each biscuit.

▲ **10.** Using the pot holders, place the cookie sheet in the oven. Set the timer and bake the biscuits for 12 minutes.

11. While the biscuits are baking, prepare the fruit filling and whipped cream.

▲ **12.** *To prepare the fruit filling,* rinse the strawberries with running cold water. Pat them dry.

Place them on the washed cutting board. With the paring knife, remove and discard the stems.

Cut each strawberry lengthwise into slices. Put the slices in the other mixing bowl.

▲ **13.** Place the peaches on the cutting board. Using the vegetable peeler, peel off and discard the skins.

With the paring knife, cut each peach in half lengthwise, starting at the stem end.

Using your fingers, remove and discard each pit.

Place each half, flat side down, on the cutting board. With the paring knife, cut each peach half lengthwise into thin slices. Put the slices in the mixing bowl with the strawberries.

14. Pour the sugar over the fruit. With the spoon, gently stir the mixture until it is well combined. Set the fruit filling aside.

▲ **15.** *To prepare the whipped cream,* pour the heavy cream into the mixer bowl. Add the vanilla extract and the sugar. With the mixer set at medium speed, beat the heavy cream until soft peaks form—that is, until the heavy cream becomes thick and fluffy and falls in soft mounds when you turn off the mixer and pull the beaters out of the heavy cream. Set the whipped cream aside.

▲ **16.** When the timer for the biscuits goes off, begin testing them for doneness by see-ing if they are golden brown (see page 22 for complete instructions).

When the biscuits are fully baked, turn off the oven. Using the pot holders, remove the cookie sheet from the oven and place it on a cooling rack.

Holding an end of the cookie sheet with a pot holder, use the pancake turner to remove the biscuits one at a time. Place each biscuit on the other cooling rack to cool completely.

▲ **17.** To serve, place the biscuits on the washed cutting board. With the paring knife, slice each one horizontally in half. Place a biscuit bottom, cut side up, on each dessert plate.

Spoon some fruit filling and its juice on each biscuit bottom. Next spoon some whipped cream on top of the fruit filling. Then place a biscuit top gently on top of the whipped cream.

Glossaries

◆ ◆ ◆ ◆ ◆ ◆ ◆ ◆ ◆ ◆ ◆ ◆

COOKING TERMS

UTENSILS

COOKING TERMS

As you prepare the recipes in this cookbook, you will come across a number of different cooking terms and will use a number of different kinds of cooking procedures. This section explains the cooking terms used in the recipes. It also gives you step-by-step directions for the cooking procedures.

Al dente an Italian phrase that means "to the tooth," or that the cooked macaroni has a little firmness when it is bitten into.

Beat to stir ingredients together rapidly in a circular motion in order to smooth out a batter or to lighten a mixture by adding air. Beating can be done using a wooden spoon, a wire whisk, or an electric mixer. (See also pages 9–10.)

Boil to heat a liquid until it has reached the boiling point, which is about 212° F. A liquid that is boiling will be in constant motion and will have bubbles rising rapidly to the surface and breaking. To bring a liquid quickly to a boil, turn up the heat to high. If something begins to boil that should not, turn down the heat. (See also page 7.)

Chop to cut food into small, irregular pieces. To chop, place the food, flat side down, on the cutting board and hold it firmly in place with one hand. Hold a paring knife firmly with the other hand. Cut the food lengthwise into small strips. Then gather the strips together and, holding them firmly, cut them crosswise into small pieces. The pieces can be unevenly shaped, but the size of the pieces should be fairly uniform so that they cook at the same rate. If they aren't, some of the pieces will be fully cooked and others will not be. (See also pages 3–4.)

Combine to mix two or more ingredients together so they are evenly distributed.

Crosswise across. To cut crosswise, place the food, flat side down, on the cutting board and hold it firmly in place with one hand. Hold a paring knife with the other hand. Cut the food along its width from side to side. (See also pages 3–4.)

Dice to cut a food into small cubes about ¼-inch square. To dice, place the food, flat side down, on the cutting board and hold it firmly in place with one hand. Hold a paring knife firmly with the other hand. Cut the food lengthwise into strips. Then gather the strips together and, holding them firmly, cut them crosswise into cubes. The size of the pieces should be fairly uniform so that they cook at the same rate. If they aren't, some of the pieces will be fully cooked and others will not be. (See also pages 3–4.)

Floweret as in *broccoli floweret*. Broccoli is a deep green vegetable that comes in groupings of tiny buds attached to thick paler green stems. To turn a bunch of broccoli into flowerets, place the broccoli on the cutting board and hold it firmly in place with one hand. Hold a paring knife firmly with the other hand. Cut off most of the thick stems, leaving about ½ inch of stem attached to the buds. These flowerets can then be measured and used in recipes as needed. Do not discard the stems, because they can also be used. Peel them with a vegetable peeler. Then slice or dice them with a paring knife. The stems can then be measured and used in recipes as needed. (See also pages 3–4.)

Fold to mix in such a way as to distribute a light, airy ingredient, such as beaten egg whites, throughout a heavier mixture, such as flour, without deflating the lighter ingredient. To fold, place the lighter mixture on top of the heavier one in a bowl. Then, starting from one side of the bowl, use a rubber spatula to cut down through the center of the mixture vertically.

Scrape the spatula across the bottom of the bowl and up the other side.

As you do this, gently lift the bottom mixture and turn it over onto the top mixture. Give the bowl a quarter turn and repeat this procedure until everything is well combined.

Grate to take a large piece of food and reduce it to small pieces or thin shreds. Grating can be done using a number of different utensils, such as a metal box type of grater, a food processor, a blender, or an electric minichopper. To prepare the recipes in this cookbook, you should use the box type of grater. This type of grater has a handle at the top for a sure grip. Each side of the box is perforated with different size holes or slits. In the recipes you will be told which side of the grater to use.

When a recipe calls for "grated peel," such as orange peel, place the grater on a piece of waxed paper. Then, holding the handle of the grater firmly with one hand and the fruit in the other hand, rub the fruit along the medium-size holes of the grater. Rub gently so that you remove only the colored part of the peel. Turn the fruit frequently so that you continue to rub only the colored part of the peel. The grater will reduce the peel to small particles. (See also page 4.)

Grease to coat the surface of a pan, such as a cake pan, muffin pan, or cookie sheet, with shortening, butter, margarine, or nonstick cooking spray in order to prevent the food prepared in it from sticking.

Knead to mix a dough until it forms a smooth and pliable mass. Kneading can be done by hand or by machine. In this cookbook, you will be kneading by hand. To knead by hand, press down into the dough with the heel of your hand while pushing the dough away from your body.

Then fold the dough over, and give it a quarter turn. Repeat this pressing-folding-turning process for the amount of time called for in the recipe, or until the dough feels smooth and satiny.

Lengthwise the longest dimension of an object. To cut lengthwise, place the food, flat side down, on the cutting board and hold it firmly in place with one hand. Hold a paring knife firmly with the other hand. Cut the food along its length from top to bottom. (See also pages 3–4.)

Marinate to soak in a marinade. A marinade is a mixture of seasonings, an acid (such as vinegar, lemon juice, or wine), and sometimes oil. A marinade is used to enhance the flavor of the food or as a means of tenderizing it.

Mash to smash or crush a food, such as a cooked potato, into an evenly textured mixture. Mashing can be done using a potato masher. To mash, grip the potato masher by the handle, and use an up-and-down motion to crush or smash the food into smaller and smaller pieces until it is the texture called for in the recipe.

Packed a measuring term that is often used with such ingredients as fresh basil leaves, parsley leaves, and spinach leaves, as well as with brown sugar. When a recipe calls for a packed measurement, put the ingredient in the measuring cup or spoon, press down on the ingredient, and continue to add more of it until there is no room left in the cup or spoon. This term is the opposite of *loosely packed*. When a recipe calls for a loosely packed measurement, put just enough of the ingredient in the measuring cup or spoon and do *not* press down on it. (See also pages 13–14.)

Pan-Fry a method of cooking food in an uncovered skillet using a small amount of fat; also called sautéing. There are other types of frying methods, based upon the amount of fat used, but in this cookbook, you will be pan-frying food. To fry food successfully, make sure the oil is hot. A good indication that the oil is hot enough is the sizzling sound it makes when a small amount of food comes in contact with it. If the oil is not hot, the food will stick to the bottom of the skillet, the outside of the food will not sear—or brown—and juices will escape. Also, do not crowd the skillet with too much food. If there is not enough space around the pieces of food, they will steam rather than brown. (See also pages 5–6 and 8.)

Peel to remove the peel from a fruit or the skin from a vegetable. Peeling can be done using a vegetable peeler. There are several types available, but the kind with the swivel blade is best because the blade follows the contours of the food being peeled. To peel, place the food on the cutting board and hold it firmly in place with one hand. Hold the vegetable peeler firmly with the other hand. Place the peeler near the hand holding the food. Then, moving the vegetable peeler *away* from you, run it along the length of the food. Remove the piece of peel. Place the peeler back at the starting position and continue to remove the peel, turning the food until the peel has been completely removed. When you become more comfortable using the vegetable peeler, you may run the peeler back and forth along the length of the food in a continuous motion, while turning the food, until the peel has been completely removed. (See also page 4.)

Pinch a measuring term used to describe the amount of a dry ingredient, such as salt or pepper, that can be held between the thumb and forefinger. A pinch is equal to about 1/16 teaspoon.

Preheat   to heat an oven to a specific temperature before placing the food inside. (See also pages 17–18.)

Rounded   a measuring term that refers to filling a measuring cup or a measuring spoon until the ingredient is slightly higher than the edge of the cup or spoon. (See also page 14.)

Sauté   see Pan-Fry.

Scoop   to cut a food into round or oval pieces. Scooping can be done using a melon baller. This utensil consists of a handle with two different-size round or oval bowls at either end. To scoop, hold the melon baller firmly with one hand and the food firmly with the other hand. Press one of the bowls down into the flesh of the food and

turn the handle to scoop out a ball of food. A melon baller can also be used to scoop out the core and seeds of a fruit, such as an apple. (See also page 153.)

Shred   to cut food into thin strips. Shredding can be done using a number of different utensils, such as a knife, a flat or metal box type of grater, or a food processor fitted with a shredding disk. To prepare the recipes in this cookbook, you should use the box type of grater (see Grate). In the recipes you will be told which side of the grater to use. When a recipe calls for "shredded vegetables or cheese," place the grater on a piece of waxed paper or in a mixing bowl. Then, holding the handle of the grater firmly with one hand and the food in the other hand, gently rub the food along the side of the grater with the largest holes. The grater will reduce the food to long, thin strips or ribbons. (See also page 4.)

Simmer   to heat a liquid to just below the boiling point, or to about 185° F. A liquid that is simmering is heated so that tiny bubbles begin to form, gently rise to the surface, and barely break. Simmering is a slow method of cooking used in preparing soups and stews. (See also page 7.)

Slice to cut into flat pieces. To slice, place the food, flat side down, on the cutting board and hold it firmly in place with one hand. Hold a paring knife firmly with the other hand. Cut the food into lengthwise or crosswise pieces as the recipe directs. The size of the pieces should be fairly uniform so that they cook at the same rate. If they aren't, some of the pieces will be fully cooked and others will not be. (See also pages 3–4.)

Soften to leave butter or margarine at room temperature until it reaches the consistency at which it can be easily spread.

Steep to soak a substance, such as tea leaves, ground coffee, or herbs, in a hot liquid until the flavor has been removed from the substance and absorbed by the liquid.

Stir to mix in a slow circular motion in order to combine ingredients thoroughly or to keep ingredients from burning or clumping. Stirring is usually done with a spoon. While stirring, you should hold on to a side of the bowl or hold the handle of the pot or pan in order to keep the vessel steady. You should also stir slowly so the ingre-

dients do not splash or spill out; this is particularly important if the ingredients are hot and can burn your skin. Stirring needs to be done thoroughly so that all the ingredients are well combined. When a mixture contains both wet and dry ingredients, you may have to use the spoon to scrape ingredients from the side and bottom of the bowl or pan in order to blend them.

Tear a cooking term often used when greens are being prepared for a salad. To prepare torn salad greens, rip or tear the leaves into bite-size pieces with your fingers. Salad greens are often prepared this way, because torn edges will not darken as quickly as edges that have been cut with a knife.

Tender-Crisp a cooking term meaning that the vegetable should be cooked until it has lost its raw taste but is still somewhat firm.

UTENSILS

As you prepare the recipes in this cookbook, you will be using a number of different utensils. The next section shows you what they look like. The utensils are labeled so that you can find them easily.

WOODEN SPATULA

RULER

LARGE
FORK

WOODEN
SPOON

SERRATED
KNIFE

THIN RUBBER
SPATULA

RUBBER
SPATULA

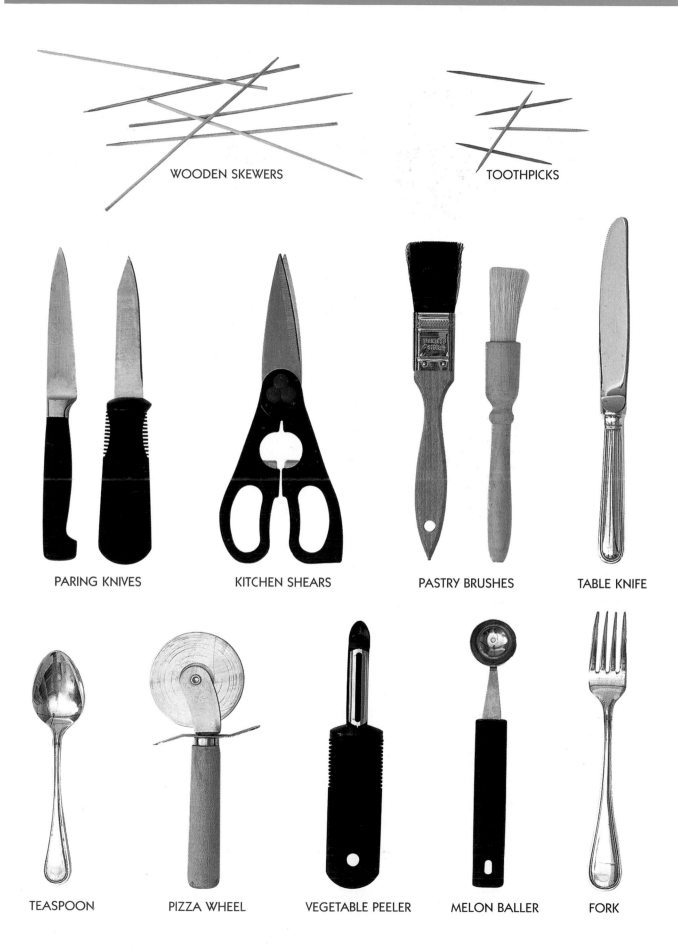

WOODEN SKEWERS

TOOTHPICKS

PARING KNIVES

KITCHEN SHEARS

PASTRY BRUSHES

TABLE KNIFE

TEASPOON

PIZZA WHEEL

VEGETABLE PEELER

MELON BALLER

FORK

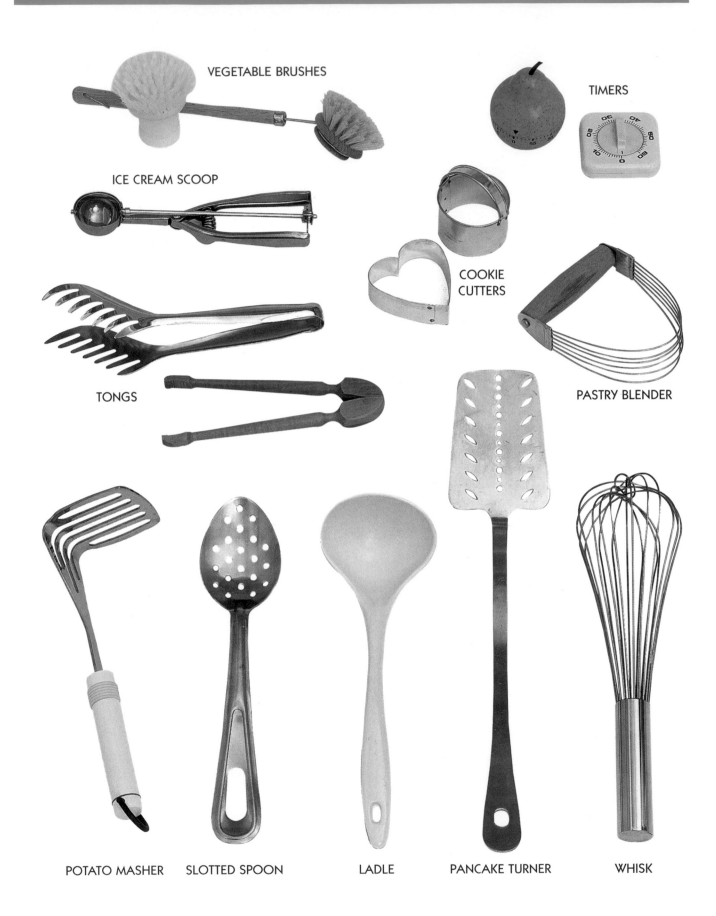

VEGETABLE BRUSHES

TIMERS

ICE CREAM SCOOP

COOKIE CUTTERS

PASTRY BLENDER

TONGS

POTATO MASHER   SLOTTED SPOON   LADLE   PANCAKE TURNER   WHISK

LIQUID MEASURING CUPS

SUNDAE GLASS

BOX GRATER

WIDE-BOTTOMED GLASS

DRY MEASURING CUPS

INSTANT-READ THERMOMETER

OVEN THERMOMETER

MEAT THERMOMETER

MEASURING SPOONS

SALAD SPINNER

LARGE MIXING BOWLS

SMALL MIXING BOWLS

CUTTING BOARDS

COLANDER

STRAINER

SAUCEPOT WITH LID

SKILLET WITH LID

NONSTICK SKILLET

ROASTING PAN

SAUCEPAN WITH LID

TEA KETTLE

MUFFIN PAN

JELLY-ROLL PAN

COOKIE SHEET

LOAF PAN

CASSEROLE

BAKING DISH

PIE PLATE

BAKING PAN

PIZZA PAN

FOOD PROCESSOR
WITH KNIFE BLADE

BLENDER

ELECTRIC MIXER

HAND-HELD
ELECTRIC MIXER

COOLING RACKS

CAN OPENER

TRIVET

ROASTING RACK

CUPCAKE LINERS

STORAGE CONTAINERS

ALUMINUM FOIL

WAXED PAPER

PLASTIC WRAP

OVEN MITTS

POT HOLDER

SEALABLE FOOD STORAGE BAGS